Samantha Gordon's Winning Season

Sweet Feet

Samantha Gordon's Winning Season

SAMANTHA GORDON

WITH **ARI BRUENING**

FOREWORD BY **ABBY WAMBACH**

WALKER BOOKS FOR YOUNG READERS
AN IMPRINT OF BLOOMSBURY
NEW YORK   LONDON   NEW DELHI   SYDNEY

First published in the United States of America in October 2013
by Walker Books for Young Readers, an imprint of Bloomsbury Publishing, Inc.
www.bloomsbury.com

For information about permission to reproduce selections from this book, write to
Permissions, Walker BFYR, 1385 Broadway, New York, New York 10018
Bloomsbury books may be purchased for business or promotional use. For information
on bulk purchases please contact Macmillan Corporate and Premium Sales Department at
specialmarkets@macmillan.com

Library of Congress Cataloging-in-Publication Data
Gordon, Samantha.
Sweet feet : Samantha Gordon's winning season / by Samantha Gordon with Ari Bruening.
pages   cm.
Summary: Ten-year-old Samantha "Sweet Feet" Gordon isn't just a girl who plays football.
She's also the best player in a league full of boys and has become an online sensation.
ISBN 978-0-8027-3715-1 (paperback) • ISBN 978-0-8027-3654-3 (hardcover)
ISBN 978-0-8027-3655-0 (e-book)
1. Gordon, Samantha, 2003– —Juvenile literature. 2. Women football players—
United States—Biography—Juvenile literature. 3. Child celebrities—
United States—Biography—Juvenile literature. I. Bruening, Ari. II. Title.
GV939.G665A3 2013   796.332092—dc23   [B]   2013019855

Book design by Yelena Safranova
Printed and bound in the U.S.A. by Thomson-Shore Inc., Dexter, Michigan
2 4 6 8 10 9 7 5 3 1 (paperback)
2 4 6 8 10 9 7 5 3 1 (hardcover)

All papers used by Bloomsbury Publishing, Inc., are natural, recyclable products
made from wood grown in well-managed forests. The manufacturing processes
conform to the environmental regulations of the country of origin.

Samantha Gordon's Winning Season

FOREWORD

When I first heard about Sam Gordon's highlight video, like many others who have seen her running for touchdown after touchdown, getting plowed over by boys—and popping right back up again!—I was amazed. You can't help but enjoy seeing that ponytail dangling out the back of her helmet as she eludes would-be tacklers and sprints into the end zone.

I was immediately struck by two thoughts. First: Sam was sending a great message that girls are capable of competing with boys in traditionally male sports. Second: That even against all odds and despite many people's opinions that she should not be playing football at all, Sam was doing what she loved and what would allow her to grow into the person she wanted to be.

I soon learned that Sam not only played soccer, as well as football, but that Alex Morgan and I were two of her favorite soccer players. I knew I had to meet this girl. So I invited Sam and her family to a US Women's National Team game in Arizona.

As soon as my teammates and I met Sam, we could tell that her confidence and magnetic personality were beyond her young years. In front of twenty women she's watched play soccer on television, Sam wasn't nervous at all—quite the opposite. She was outgoing and comfortable talking to everyone, to the point that a few of us were slightly taken aback by how composed and mature she was. Equally impressive was how she was handling her sudden celebrity. Seeing Sam play football and meeting her at our training session reminded me that when you approach a situation with confidence, whether on the field or in life, you are at your purest and best.

The women on the US team are in the position of being role models for young people, so we understand how important it is to connect with fans. Sam has that naturally. It was incredibly special for me to meet a talented and strong female who is in a small way reshaping what it means to be an athlete. Sometimes it takes a special individual doing something extraordinary for society to really take notice.

Sam is fearless, and she doesn't even realize how special she is, because she's just doing what comes naturally to her. It's as if no one ever told Sam that girls usually don't play football, and when she did, the world marveled at her feats. That's a wonderful thing. Just over forty years after the passing of Title IX, which prohibits gender discrimination in athletics, this is our reality: Sam Gordon didn't see any reason why she couldn't play the sport she loved.

The example Sam sets goes far beyond the field of play. She is funny, adorable, and always smiling, but also humble, and a mentally tough and tremendously competitive winner. Everyone—athlete or not, male or female—can learn from her approach to life. No matter what the challenge, Sam meets it head-on for the right reason: because it's just plain fun.

Abby Wambach
US Women's National Soccer Team

INTRODUCTION

Where No Gremlin Leaguer Has Gone Before

"Every time she saw a video of you, Sam, my little four-year-old daughter . . . kept saying, 'Girls' team! Girls' team!'"
—Josh Elliott, *Good Morning America* anchor

I was scared. It was my first football game, and my coach had decided to make me the team's starting quarterback. The first play Coach Staib called was for me to run with the ball. I took a deep breath. I knew I could do this. I had been practicing for weeks. So far no other player could catch me in practice. But this wasn't a drill, and I didn't know what would happen in a real game. My heart was pounding as I ran onto the field and lined up. I could hear the crowd yelling on the sidelines, but I had no idea what they were saying, because I was focused only on the ball that was about to be hiked to me. What if I didn't catch it? What if a tackler knocked it out of my hands? I couldn't let my team down. As I lifted my hands in front of my face to catch the ball, I couldn't keep them from shaking.

I signaled to my teammate, and he hiked the ball back to me. I made sure I kept my eyes on the ball until it was in my hands before I started to run. I took off to the right, where I knew my teammates would be blocking for me. A player from the other team was waiting there to tackle me. I stopped, faked left, and cut right, and his arms caught nothing but air. My blockers kept the other defenders away from me, and I broke through the first line of the defense. Then I heard my coach yelling, "Get to the outside! Get to the outside!" So I ran to the edge of the field as fast as I could.

A tackler was sprinting toward the sideline where I was headed, trying to cut me off. I told my legs to go even faster, and somehow they listened. With an

Including this first one, I scored twenty-five touchdowns in one season!

extra burst of speed, I flew past the boy before he could get to me. Now I was ahead of everybody in the open field, with the defenders chasing me. My body was telling me it couldn't go any farther, but I ignored it and kept running. Nobody caught me before I crossed the goal line. That's right: I ran the entire length of the field for a touchdown the very first time I got the ball! I wanted to jump up and down and celebrate, but I knew that wasn't allowed, so I just gave the ball to the referee and walked back to my team.

I didn't need to jump and scream anyway, because other people were doing it for me. One of the assistant coaches had been running down the sideline, following me and hopping up and down. My teammates swarmed around me, yelling and high-fiving me left and right. It was a hot August day, and I was sweaty and tired, but I was so happy that I didn't mind. All the hard work we'd put in every day in practice was totally worth it!

That touchdown was just the first of many. Even I never expected to play as well as I did. When people see a girl playing so well with her ponytail hanging out of her helmet, they're usually really surprised, and that makes me smile. Nobody ever expects a girl to be so good at playing football with boys, and I don't blame them, because people have told me I might be accomplishing something no other girl has done before.

More important than scoring touchdowns, though,

was winning football games. What mattered most to me was doing my part so my team, the Herriman Mustangs, did well. My teammates blocked the defenders for me, and my coach taught us a lot, about football and about life. He also created the plays we ran. Together we ended up tied for first place in our division! That was a lot of fun, and I liked being part of something bigger than myself.

Most Valuable Player Indeed

Sam "Sweet Feet" Gordon finished the season with the kind of jaw-dropping statistics that NFL Most Valuable Player Adrian Peterson can only wish for:

- **Carries**: 232
- **Yards**: 1,911 yards
- **Yards per carry**: 8.2
- **Total Scores**: 35
- **Touchdowns**: 25
- **Tackles**: 65
- **Fumbles**: 1

I was just playing football the best I could, but other people thought I was doing something special. After the season ended, my dad posted to the Internet a four-minute video of my highlights showing me using my "sweet feet" to run away from the other kids. Within a few hours, *The Ellen DeGeneres Show* and *Good Morning America* called, wanting to do stories about me. Within three days, the video had almost five million views. Within a month, I'd been on nine national television programs and spent far more time traveling around the country meeting sports and TV celebrities than I did at home. Literally overnight, I'd become famous, and it didn't stop at the borders of the United States—a film crew from one of the biggest TV programs in Japan even came to my house.

Complete strangers now recognize me. I've signed autographs more times than I can count. One of my two favorite experiences (so far) happened when NFL Commissioner Roger Goodell invited me to the Super

I attended Super Bowl XLVII in New Orleans, Louisiana, and even starred in a commercial during the game.

Bowl, where I watched the game in his luxury box with people like New Jersey Governor Chris Christie; Super Bowl champion coach Tony Dungy; and the family of the Harbaugh brothers, who were coaching the two Super Bowl teams. Before the game, I got to hang out with a lot of celebrities, and I even did a skit on the NFL Honors award show. At the Super Bowl, 108 million people saw me and a short clip of my highlights!

My other favorite experience was when Abby Wambach invited me to a soccer practice and game with the US Women's National Team, where I got to meet Abby, Alex Morgan, and the rest of the team. My dream is to play soccer on the Women's National Team in the Olympics, and Abby and Alex are two of my biggest heroes. They were very nice to me. I'll never forget spending so much time with them.

The US Women's National Team won the gold medal in the 2008 and 2012 Olympics. I love to play soccer when I'm not playing football.

I'd always wanted to be famous, but I didn't really think it would ever happen. Who knew that playing football would put me on national television with Alec Baldwin and Shaquille O'Neal and on the front of a Wheaties box? I guess people just aren't used to seeing a girl play ball like I do. But I don't think my story is just about me. It's about what we can accomplish even when other people think we can't. I want people who hear my story to not be afraid to try hard things. And remember: when you're chasing your dream, it doesn't matter if you're a boy or a girl.

CHAPTER 1
A Tommy Boy?

"I want Sam to grow up really strong and self-confident and feel like she can compete and that nobody can tell her that her place is here or there."
—Brent Gordon, Sam's father

I'll never forget the boy at school who smiled at me and said, "Sam, you're a Tommy boy." It was Halloween and I was dressed as an army soldier. If a Tommy boy is someone who likes sports and is okay playing with boys, then that's me. I thought that was a pretty cool name for it. I could tell he thought being a Tommy boy was a good thing, so I took it as a compliment. In a lot of ways, though, I'm just like other girls, and I play with them a lot too—I like to play with anyone who loves to run fast, climb high, and have fun.

You could even say I have a Tommy boy name. My parents named me Sam because they wanted me to have a name that wasn't too "girly," one that could work for either a boy or a girl, so it came down to Alex or Sam. I guess they hoped my name could teach me that I can do anything I want, that I don't just have to do things girls are "supposed" to do. Just in case I turned out to be really girly, they officially named me Samantha so I could use that name if I wanted to, but I've always just been Sam.

When I was three years old, we moved from Salt Lake City, Utah, to Blackfoot, Idaho, which is known as the Potato Capital of the World. It's a very small town, but the area grows more potatoes than anywhere else. Blackfoot also has the Idaho Potato Museum, where there's a huge fake potato, topped with butter and sour cream, that's taller than a person. My neighborhood was surrounded by potato fields.

Not very long after we moved to Idaho, my parents got divorced, and that was really hard for me. After the divorce, for the next two years I was the only girl with three boys in the house: my dad and my two brothers, Max and Ben. Max is three years older than me, and Ben is three years younger. None of the boys in my family treated me any different because I was a girl. My good friend Kendall lived next door, and he is also a boy. I'd go outside and play soccer or hide-and-seek or tag or basketball with Kendall, Max, and Kendall's older brother Avery, who was Max's friend. Sometimes other kids in the neighborhood, most of them boys, would play with us, but usually it was just the four of us. When he had time, my dad would come out and play soccer with us in our yard.

I was just one of the boys with my older brother, Max, and my little brother, Ben.

Hardly anybody lives in Blackfoot, and there are lots of really big spaces. Our family had a huge yard filled with grass and pine trees, and even our own little basketball court. We played outside almost all the time. Kids in our neighborhood had Nerf guns and bikes. We could go in the neighbors' yards too, and there were even a trampoline and a playhouse in the neighborhood that we liked to play with. Sometimes we'd play a game where Max and his friend tried to catch Kendall and me.

There was a tall tree in the yard that I liked to climb, even though my dad worried it wasn't safe. I'd climb really high, almost as high as our house. I'd go up there whenever I wanted some time alone. Max couldn't climb it, and neither could Ben, unless Max or I helped him up to the first branch. I even took a pencil and a notepad and a blanket up there so I could draw. Sometimes I liked to climb out on a branch and jump over to the limb of another tree just for fun. That *really* scared my dad!

We also rode our bikes around the neighborhood.

I loved to climb the tree in my yard, even though it scared my dad.

When I was five, I had training wheels. My dad was planning to take them off and teach me to ride, but he'd been waiting until we had half a day to try because he thought it would take a long time for me to learn. One day when my dad came home from work I asked him to take the training wheels off my bike, since Kendall didn't have them on his. My dad said, "Not right now, but I'll teach you how to ride soon."

But I'd already learned to ride on Kendall's bike. I told my dad I could ride without training wheels and asked for a chance to prove it. So he said, "Okay, if you show me you can ride Kendall's bike, I'll take your training wheels off."

Sam's Favorite Things

TV shows:
Austin & Ally, Shake It Up,
Wizards of Waverly Place,
Adventure Time, and
Regular Show

Books:
the Twilight series and
the Hunger Games series

Movies:
the Twilight series and
Hunger Games

Animals:
dogs and cheetahs

Music:
Lady Gaga, Britney Spears,
Katy Perry, Ke$ha, and
Taylor Swift

iPhone apps:
Tapped Out, Bike Race,
Temple Run, and
Hungry Shark

We went outside, and I hopped on Kendall's bike and took off. I rode it without any training wheels and didn't fall! Then my dad went straight into the garage, pulled out his tools, and took off my training wheels. My dad likes to tell about how I learned to ride a bike all by myself.

When you grow up in Utah and Idaho, there are a lot of fun things to do outdoors, like camping, and beautiful places to do them. One year, all the boys in my dad's family—my uncles and cousins and brothers—were going on a camping trip while all the girls stayed with Grandma. I asked my dad if I could go camping with the boys, and he said I could! I was the only girl on the trip, but nobody minded that I was there. It was a lot of fun, even if I had to go a long way away to go to the bathroom in the woods. We fished in the lake, and I caught eleven fish! I didn't like touching the bait or the fish, so I had to have someone help me bait the hook, take the fish off, and gut the fish. I guess when it comes to fishing, I'm a *little* girly.

Since I spent a lot of time with boys in my family and neighborhood, I didn't think it was strange to play with the boys at school. In fact, that's where I first remember playing football. I was the only girl who played touch football with the boys during school recess. Nobody ever said anything to me about playing football with the boys, but at a parent-teacher conference, my teacher asked if she could talk to my

In Utah and Idaho, there's a lot to do outdoors, like camping.

dad alone. I didn't find out until much later, but my dad says she had two things to talk to him about.

First, she was worried because I played football with the boys at recess. I don't know what she thought was wrong with that, but she thought my dad should ask me to stop. A few months later, when she saw my dad again, she told him she was concerned that I was still doing it. He was fine with me playing football with the boys, so he never told me to stop, or even that my teacher thought I should. I'm glad he didn't, because I love playing football.

The other thing my teacher talked to my dad about was that I should test for the gifted and talented program. So I took the test and scored high enough to enter the program! Max and I like to joke that we are nerds because we like to read and do math and science. But we think being a nerd is a good thing.

Quick in Every Subject

"Sam is a hard worker, very likable, offers to help when she sees a need, is very calm, and is honestly a friend to everybody! She's very quick in every subject, I suppose just like her feet!"
—Alessandra Meyer, Sam's fourth-grade teacher

I took first place in my third-grade science fair and my class spelling bee, but my favorite subject is

I've always been a good student.

reading. In math, I already know most of what we're learning. Max has always been willing to teach me what he's learning in school. When I tried to get into the gifted and talented program, he taught me how to add and subtract and worked with me on other subjects that would be on the test. He's so smart that his teacher once gave him a textbook to read and do the problems on his own, since he was so far ahead of everyone else.

Max and the other boys weren't the only friends I had. I also had a good friend named Halle. I mostly just played with her at school because she lived far away on a farm. Whenever she and I had recess at the same time, we'd play games together. We played tag with other girls, or we'd get a big group of kids together to play a game we called Rabbit and Fox. One kid would be the fox and try to catch the other kids, who were the rabbits. Halle and I were two of the fastest kids, so we stuck together and were often the last ones to get caught.

I also played soccer at school. Sometimes I tried playing with a group of fifth graders. I could tell they didn't expect a second grader to be as good as them. They thought I'd be really timid and scared, but I wasn't. I went after the ball and played hard against them, and after a while, they accepted me as part of the group. It made me feel good that I could do well against older kids.

My days being surrounded mostly by boys ended

when my dad remarried. I was almost seven years old. Instead of just three boys and me, we now had two more girls in the house: my stepmom, Brooke, and my little sister, Annie, who is two years younger than me. I was used to being one of the boys, and I didn't know what to expect. Annie is a lot different from me. She likes to play with dolls and dress up like a princess. She had a big princess castle, princess dresses, pretend makeup and jewelry, and a big dollhouse. I didn't want to play with any of that.

I like stuffed animals, but I've never been into dolls. I don't think my parents ever gave me any. When my grandpa gave me a doll for Christmas, I never even opened it; Annie was the first one to play with it, two years later. If I'd opened it, my brothers probably would have used her as a target for their Nerf guns anyway.

I've never been into princesses and dresses much either. When I was really little, I was a princess for Halloween, but it was so cold in Blackfoot that I had to wear long johns under my dress. Other than that one time, I don't remember ever wanting to dress up as a princess or play with princess stuff. So when Annie brought all her dolls and princess dresses to the house, it was very different from what I'd grown up with so far.

Even though Brooke and Annie don't like sports as much as I do, they're still great to have around.

Every day is fun at the Gordon household.

They really feel like family now. Ben and Annie have become good friends, and my stepmom is one of my biggest fans. She drives all of us around to our sports practices, makes sure we eat good meals and snacks to have enough energy, brings our uniforms and water, and cheers for me more than anyone else does.

After my dad remarried, we all moved back to the Salt Lake City area in Utah. Our yard is a *lot* smaller now, and the neighborhood we live in is new, so the trees aren't big enough to climb. I miss climbing trees. But there are some really great things about my new neighborhood, like parks and trails and even a small lake! The movie theater is nearby too, so we go to the movies a lot. And best of all, we are closer to my grandma, who is a great cook and makes us dinner every Sunday.

My family likes to play sports together in the park or at a gym that's close to our house. I still remember one time we played football as a family at the park. Max and I were on one team, and we played against my dad and stepmom. Max got the ball and started running down the field until it looked like Dad was about to get him. He pitched the ball to me, and I took off until Brooke got close, then I tossed the ball back to him. We pitched the football back and forth four or five times before we scored a touchdown. The look on my dad's face was awesome! I think some of my competitive spirit comes from him.

No Ordinary Kid

"Sam is no ordinary kid. She has this ability to think about others. After dinner, all the kids will go play, and Sam will be the only one to ask if I need any help cleaning up. I'll tell her she doesn't need to help me, but she'll say, 'Well, I feel bad that we're all playing while you're just cleaning. I think I need to help you.'"

—Brooke Gordon, Sam's stepmother

I still play soccer, football, and tag at recess. A lot of my friends are girls now that we've moved back to Salt

Lake City. I'll play with anyone who likes the same kinds of things I do, whether they're a boy or a girl. Especially sports. If that makes me a Tommy boy, I don't have a problem with that.

CHAPTER 2

All Kinds of Sports

"This young lady rocks! Not just a fantastic athlete, but a FANTASTIC person . . . the perfect example of good sportsmanship!"
—Comment from a fan on espn.com

I first played sports for a real team when I was seven, but I learned to be competitive and tough long before that. Max never went easy on me when we played in the yard together. He's really competitive and does *not* like to lose, so he played pretty aggressively sometimes. Sometimes my dad even had to put him in time-out for being too rough. But I didn't let him get to me. I always tried my hardest against him.

Having an older brother who played hard trained me to be tough and not be intimidated by boys. When Max, Kendall, Avery, and I played sports, our rule was that we couldn't cry unless we had a broken bone, and I always followed that rule, even if I got hurt.

Now my brother and I don't play together as much because we play in organized leagues. Max began playing league sports a few years before I did. He started with soccer, and then, when he was old enough, he got into football. As for me, I'll try any sport. I even tried baseball for one season. There are times when I have to be at practice or a game just about every day. Sometimes I'll have a soccer game in the morning and a basketball game in the after- noon. Those are really fun days. I had to quit baseball because the practices and games were at the same time as my soccer practices and games, and soccer won out for me.

A Day in the Life of Sam Gordon

- **School:** 8:30 a.m.–3:25 p.m.
- **Homework:** 3:30–4:30 p.m.
- **Speed and agility training (wearing her soccer uniform):** 5–6 p.m.
- **Dinner while riding in the car:** 6–6:30 p.m.
- **Soccer practice:** 6:30–8 p.m.
- **After practice, it's time for bed.**

The first organized sport I played was soccer. My league in Blackfoot was coed, so the boys and girls played together. When I first met my coach, he looked more like a farmer than a soccer coach. He wore Wrangler jeans and cowboy boots instead of sweats and cleats. It just goes to show that you can't judge a book by its cover, because he really knew his soccer and was an awesome coach.

You have to be a bit hard core to play soccer in Idaho because it's still really cold when the season starts. For most of our games we had to wear coats and gloves and hats. Sometimes it even snowed during our games! I really had fun, though. One of my favorite plays I remember was when I got the ball near our own team's goal and started running down the field. A boy ran at me and crashed into me, knocking both of us down. I was used to that style of soccer after playing with Max, so I quickly popped back up and kept running with the ball—until another boy smashed into me and we both fell down. I jumped up again and kept going. Then two more boys hit me! We all crashed to the ground, but I got back to my feet and raced down the field. Now I had a wide open shot at the goal! I'd like to say I scored, but I didn't. I missed an easy shot!

I wasn't always perfect in soccer, but my dad says that was when he realized I could be really good at sports. He overheard parents on the sidelines pointing out "that tiny little girl" who was really fast. They liked to watch me because they didn't expect such a small girl to be as fast, tough, and fearless as I was. It always made me feel good after the games when the parents of the other teams' players came to tell me I did a good job. That kind of encouragement made me want to play hard.

Since we moved back to Utah, I've gotten into more

Believe it or not, my favorite sport is actually soccer.

competitive club soccer. Long before I was "Sweet Feet," one of my soccer coaches gave me a different nickname. I was "Firecracker," because I was so small but packed a big punch. The next year, a different coach called me "Mighty Mouse" for the same reason. I may not be the biggest player in any of the sports I do, but I've never been afraid to mix it up with bigger kids.

No Fear

Casey Clements, Sam's soccer coach in Blackfoot, Idaho, says he wasn't worried about her getting hurt, but he jokes, "Was I ever concerned about anybody she may mow down? Yeah. There was no fear in her."

One day I want to play for the US Women's National Team like Abby Wambach and Alex Morgan.

That dream is why I practice so hard. Football is what made me famous, and I really like it, but soccer will always be my first love.

When soccer season ends, I switch to basketball. When I started playing organized basketball in Idaho, we played with a little ball and a short basket. I remember one game where my coach matched me up against the tallest girl on the other team. She held the ball high over her head so I couldn't reach it. I did my best to guard her, and everybody waited at the other end of the court while she stood still, not daring to bring the ball down. Finally, I jumped as high as I could and smacked the ball out of her hands. Then I ran around her, got the ball, and took it to the hoop.

Like soccer, basketball has gotten more competitive for me as I've gotten older. Now I play with the Junior Jazz, a program sponsored by the Utah Jazz of the NBA. Being short is probably more of a challenge in basketball than in any other sport, but at least I'm fast. At one game, a parent even told me I had an unfair advantage because I'm short! I guess she thought if I was taller I wouldn't be as quick.

My speed helps in every sport I play. The first time I remember racing was against Max when I was five or six. Max won. One day, though, I got to the point where I was just as fast as him. After a while, I could outrun him. Sometimes we'd race as a family in the school field across the street, and I'd win. He's so competitive that

Basketball, football, soccer? You name it, I like to play it.

he'd say, "Let's have a rematch." But I'd always win the second time . . . and the third.

The first time I won an organized race was in third grade. My school has something called the Fun Run. It's a two-mile race, and I think they gave it the wrong name, because after two miles it doesn't feel fun anymore. The whole school raced, which meant that I was running against a lot of older kids, even sixth graders. I took fourth place out of the entire school, and I was the first-place girl. The only kids who were faster than me were two sixth-grade boys and one fourth-grade boy.

Since I'm so fast, one of the teachers at school

suggested I try the Hershey's Track and Field program. It's a program where the fastest kids from across the country get to go to Hershey, Pennsylvania, to race in a national track meet. It sounded fun, so I gave it a try. My first race was a local meet where I ran against about thirty girls. Some of them were nine years old, like me; others were ten. The top two runners got to move on to the next level, but I took third in both of my races. The same two girls crossed the finish line before I did in both the fifty-meter and hundred-meter races.

I guess as fast as I am, there are girls out there who are even faster. Maybe they should try football too! It just shows that no matter how good you are at sports, there might be someone out there who's better. Sports are very competitive. You have to work really hard if you want to be the best you can be. That's why the best athletes do tons of training, starting at a young age.

Max knew training is important, so after his first football season he asked my dad if he could work out with some other football players who were doing speed and agility drills. My dad asked the trainer if I could join them too, and the trainer said I could. I didn't know what I was in for!

My speed and agility trainers are pretty intense. One of them used to be a running back for the Seattle Seahawks in the NFL, and another played college football. My main trainer's name is Rocky. If you've ever seen the Rocky movies, you know how hard Rocky worked. Well, my trainer is even more hard core than that! He makes sure I'm always in great shape.

I was expecting to just run on a track and lift weights or something, but that's not what it's like at all. You do exercises like tire jumps, sleds, and obstacle courses, but they're not nearly as fun as they sound. With sleds you have to tie yourself to a sled with really heavy weights on it and run. It feels like you're trying to pull a bus behind you. We also do burpees, squats, pushups, ladders, and exercises with resistance bands. You probably don't want to know what all of those are, but take my word for it: they make your muscles turn to Jell-O

I really like my trainer, Rocky, even though his workouts are really tough.

after a while. One thing I do like is the obstacle courses. They stack up boxes and we have to run around and jump over them. That's fun.

Max and I would always tell my parents how hard speed and agility training is, but we didn't think they really believed us. So we begged them to do it with us, and my dad and stepmom both agreed to train with us on Saturdays. I probably shouldn't have enjoyed seeing my dad have to work so hard, but I did. Rocky didn't go easy on my parents at all; after we finished a session, they'd walk to the car really slowly, as if their legs didn't want to move anymore. They admitted the workouts were tough, but they kept going with us, saying that if we did, they would do it too. The family competition could get pretty intense, because if you didn't finish some of the drills first, you had to do extra exercises.

I love sports, and I'm willing to put in the extra work to be good at them. I'll try just about anything for a season or two! Soccer and basketball are great, but I never imagined I'd end up playing tackle football.

CHAPTER 3

Why Not Football?

"I'm proud of my little sister. When I told my friends that Sam Gordon was my sister, some of them didn't believe me, but those who did were really impressed."
—Max Gordon, Sam's older brother

After all that training, I wondered if I could hold my own against Max and his football teammates. Max was now playing his second season of football, and after my soccer practices my dad often took me along to pick up Max from his football practice. We usually got there as practice finished, when Max's team was running wind sprints. That means they ran as fast as they could for about twenty yards, turned around, and sprinted back until the coach told them they could stop.

I knew I could outrun Max, and I was curious how I'd do against the rest of the team, so one time I asked my dad if I could run the sprints with them. He said it was okay as long as I stayed on the sidelines and didn't get in the way.

I lined up alongside the boys for the first wind sprint. Max shot me a warning look. The coach blew his whistle, and we took off. I sprinted out as fast as

I could, made the turn, and finished ahead of not just Max, but most of his teammates. There were only a few who outran me. The more sprints we ran, the better I did. I don't think Max was too happy about being outdone by his little sister in front of his friends, but I felt pretty good about myself. After all, these boys were three years older than me. In their defense, the boys were wearing pads and had been practicing for two hours. And it probably helped Max feel better that he wasn't the only one getting shown up.

After that, I raced the boys every time I came with my dad to pick up Max. Max's coach started telling his players that they needed to try to beat me, just to motivate them. I was having a lot of fun and wondered how I'd do if I had a chance to try their other drills. Before that, I'd never thought much about playing competitive football, but now I thought, "Why not?"

I got more serious about it after one of Max's practices. I'd just finished racing the older boys when Max's coach came and talked to me. He said, "You know, Sam, I've been coaching for a long time, and I've seen girls play football. Sometimes they're the best runners on the team. You should consider playing football."

That sure got my mind going. Knowing that I could run faster than boys three years older than me made me think, "Maybe I can play." I'd also played football with boys at school often enough to know that I could hold my own, at least without pads and tackling. By the time the next season started, I would be the right age to start playing in the local league.

It took me a while to decide, because playing football meant that I would miss a lot of soccer games and practices. Football is a much more complicated game than a lot of other sports, because everyone on the team has to learn a bunch of different plays. If each player doesn't do what he (or she) is supposed to do on a particular play, it won't work. So if you miss practices, you won't know your role and your coach won't let you play very much in the game because you'll hurt your team's chances of winning. That meant I couldn't skip football for soccer.

From watching Max play, I also knew that football was much more intense than the other sports I played. For some reason, the coaches, the players, and even the parents take football really seriously. If I played, I worried there would be lots of pressure to play well. I couldn't just do it halfway—I was either all the way in or I was out.

I was following in the footsteps of my brother Max when I decided to play football. He's taught me a lot about the game.

After a lot of thought, I decided I was in. I figured soccer could wait while I did football, even though my dream was still to play professional and Olympic soccer. Besides, I could still play soccer in the spring. That wouldn't give me as much practice to hone my soccer skills, but football would at least keep me in shape.

Like most places, Utah has no football league for girls my age, so there's no choice but to play with the boys. Even if I had a choice, the big competitor in me would have chosen to go against the boys just to see how I'd do. I already had a little taste of that, and part of me wanted more.

When I told my parents about my decision, my dad didn't hesitate to say it was okay. I think he hoped I'd make that choice. My mom and stepmom didn't object, but I did find out later that they weren't quite as sure as my dad. I guess they were worried about me

My dad taught me to believe that being a girl doesn't mean I can't do what I want. He supported my decision to play football with the boys.

getting hurt. But they've been really supportive and have put in a lot of time to make it possible for me to play. I can tell they're proud of me.

Girl Trailblazers in Football

Sam is not the first girl to play football. As far back as 1939, Luverne "Toad" Wise kicked six extra points for her high school football team, and in 1998 Liz Heaston became the first woman to score in a college football game when she kicked two extra points for Oregon's Willamette University. But Sam is probably the first to become a superstar in a league of boys.

I made my decision in the fall, and tryouts for the next season didn't happen until summer, so I had plenty of time to get ready, and Max was willing to help. We have a tackling dummy at home. It's a big, heavy bag of stuffing that you can practice tackling instead of hitting a person. We used it to practice, and Max even let me try tackling him too, and taught me a lot of moves.

Rocky, my speed and agility trainer, also worked with me on football drills with the other football players he trained. We did a lot of different exercises. He set up cones and had me run through them in a certain way to learn to cut and change direction. He also set up cones in a diamond shape. I stood in one corner of the diamond, and Max stood in the other corner. Max would try to tackle me, and I had to try to get around him.

By the time tryouts came, I felt ready. But there's no way I could have prepared myself for the life-changing journey that was about to launch.

League of Their Own?

Today, there are leagues for women and girls in almost every sport, from soccer to basketball, from Little League to major league. There are a handful of women's football leagues around the country, but almost none for kids, and very few, if any, high schools offer girls' football. If a girl wants to play football, for the most part she must play with, and against, the boys.

CHAPTER 4

It Wasn't What I Wanted, but
I Wouldn't Change a Thing

"At first, it was like, 'Oh, look at that little girl in the
football outfit. She's so cute!' And then it was like,
'GO GET HER!' because she's so good."
—Katie Couric, talk-show host

I was pretty nervous about tryouts. That was partly
because, even though everyone would get picked to
play on a team, how I did at tryouts would determine
whether I'd be on one of the best teams. But it was also
because I knew that as a girl I would stand out from the
other kids. There would be a lot of people paying attention to me. Would I be able to compete against the boys?

Tryouts started on Monday, lasting for two hours
each day, and didn't end until Friday afternoon. The
coaches were supposed to get together on Friday for
the draft, which is where they pick their players. The
coaches of the top two teams, the A1 and A2 teams,
choose first and fill up their entire teams. Then the
seven B teams take turns choosing, starting with B1.
They do that so each team can match up against teams
from other districts that are on about the same skill
level. I desperately wanted to be on one of the A teams,

but I knew I'd have to work hard in the tryouts to get picked among the top players.

Playing with the Boys

"[Playing on an all-boys soccer team as a kid] was probably one of the most influential things in terms of my career. Just having that mentality of going into a game no matter who you're going to go up against . . . the ability to switch your mindset to just play your own game and play the best that you can play and almost play fearless."

—Abby Wambach, Olympic and professional soccer player, who was moved from a girls' team to a boys' team after scoring twenty-seven goals in three games

---

The biggest youth football program in the Salt Lake area is the Ute Conference. In my local division, the Herriman District, there were 172 eight- and nine-year-old kids trying out for my age group, the Gremlins. Only two of us were girls. They broke us into groups of about fifteen kids. The biggest kids, or the kids who had played before, were put into the first groups so the coaches of the top teams could evaluate them first. Since I was one of the smallest and had no experience, I wasn't in those groups. Each of the coaches ran a station where one group at a time ran a drill to test our speed and agility or show off our blocking and tackling skills.

There were a lot of speed and agility tests, but

nobody was faster than me in any of them. The coaches wanted to see how quickly we could run forward and then backward to where we started. Sometimes the coach who was running the stopwatch acted like he didn't believe my time and would ask me to run it again. Then he showed the time to another coach. There was one boy who tied with me in one of the drills. He wanted a rematch so he could be the only person with a faster time than me all week, but it never happened.

I was good in the tackling drills too. I think it's because I wasn't afraid to hit. A lot of kids hesitate right before contact and brace themselves. Not me. I just keep going as hard as I can, even though I'm one of the smallest players. Sometimes it would hurt to get hit by one of the bigger players, but I didn't mind. I was used to playing rough with Max and other boys, and contact didn't bother me.

During tryouts, nobody objected to a girl playing football, and nobody ever said there was anything wrong with it. But some parents acted like they didn't want their boys to be outplayed by a girl. One of the drills was a lot like the exercises I'd done with Rocky and Max. The cones were set up in a diamond shape, and I had the ball. I faced off against a boy who was supposed to tackle me. I faked left but went right. When I saw that the boy went the same direction, I cut back the other way, leaving him facedown in the grass.

The boy's father ran onto the field, grabbed his son's face mask, and yelled, "You don't let a girl beat you! You can't let this happen! You need to get back in there and try harder!" The boy looked embarrassed but walked back to his spot to repeat the drill. I got past him again. It felt good to do so well, but I was worried that the boy felt like he had let his dad down.

That wasn't the only time something like that happened. Lots of fathers, and even a mother or two, told their boys not to lose to a girl. I know those parents just wanted their sons to do well and were only trying to motivate them, but the boys were trying as hard as they could already, and all their parents did was make them feel bad—and teach them girls aren't supposed to be as good as boys at sports. I think it's okay for a girl to do better than a boy, just like it's okay for a boy to outdo a girl.

A lot of the coaches thought I was outdoing most of the boys. On the second day, we played Sharks and Minnows at Coach Chris Staib's station. Three kids were the sharks, and the rest of us were minnows who had to try to run past them. If we got touched, we were out. I'm pretty good at avoiding being touched. In fact, I was the last one standing almost every time we played.

Coach Staib was impressed. He said to another coach, "That girl has some sweet feet." Somehow, that nickname stuck. After the second day of practice,

We ran tons of drills for tryouts that we would later do in practice. It was a lot of running, but all that training meant I was ready.

Coach Staib came up to me and said, "I want you on my team. I'm going to do everything I can to get you." Besides my speed and ability to make people miss, he was impressed that when we were playing Sharks and Minnows, I'd run behind two of the other kids and let them get caught while I made it through. He thought that was a lot like following lead blockers who hold off the other team's tacklers while you run through with the ball. It made me really happy to know that he wanted me, even though he was the B5 coach and I was hoping to be on one of the better teams.

Before long, there was a crowd of coaches and parents around me while I was doing the drills. Even the A1 coach came over to watch me. Some of the parents started asking my stepmom if I'd played before and said they couldn't believe how well I was doing. More than one coach told her I was "A1 material." Another coach said there was no way I would go lower than B1.

Toward the end of tryouts, the A2 coach even

came up to me and asked, "Would you like to be my quarterback?"

That was exactly what I wanted to hear, so of course I told him, "Yes!" By this time, I had really high hopes that I would be picked for one of the top teams.

After tryouts ended on Friday, the coaches held the draft. We were supposed to get a call Friday night or Saturday morning to tell us what team we were on, and we were told that most teams would practice on Saturday. I felt like I was sitting on pins and needles. Would one of the top coaches choose me? I hate waiting, especially when I want to find out how good people think I am.

No call came Friday night. I couldn't sleep a wink. I kept thinking about the draft. Who would my coach be? Would I like him? Saturday morning also went by without a call. I started to wonder if there was some mistake. What if I'd slipped through the cracks and I wasn't on anybody's team at all? Or maybe I had a coach but he had forgotten to call me.

Finally, my coach called. It was Chris Staib, the one who named me Sweet Feet. He was the coach of the B5 team, which meant that about eighty players were picked before Coach Staib took me. There were six coaches who chose before he did. I was crushed that none of those six coaches wanted me. Maybe I hadn't looked as good in tryouts as I'd thought.

I remember sitting down with my dad in the

kitchen. My eyes were tearing up, but I was trying not to cry. "Dad, what happened?" I asked. "I thought you said I'd be on one of the best teams."

It took him a minute to say anything. "Sam," he finally said, "the only reason I can come up with is that you're a girl. I can't explain it any other way."

I'd never thought before that someone would treat me differently because I was a girl. I was shocked. "You mean someone wouldn't pick me just because I'm a girl? Really?"

That's when he explained to me what a stereotype is. A stereotype is when somebody assumes you'll be a certain way just because you're a girl or because your skin is a certain color or because of the way you dress or because of your religion. He said that the coaches must have assumed I won't like hitting and getting hit, or that I might get hurt easily because I'm a girl.

I can't imagine a better coach for me than Coach Staib.

Maybe, he suggested, the other coaches passed on me because they couldn't be sure I would be okay in a football game with lots of hitting.

I guess I'll never really know the reason I didn't get picked very high, but I was devastated. "Dad," I said, "I'm going to prove to everyone that I'm better than where I was picked. And I'm going to make Coach Staib glad that he chose me."

What I didn't know then was that I'd be glad he chose me too. The very first time Coach Staib talked to my dad after he picked me, he could tell my dad was upset about how low I'd fallen in the draft. He said, "Listen, I picked Sam as my number-one pick after I took my own son. I thought that Sam performed the best during tryouts of any runner who came through my station. I really, really wanted her on my team, and I don't care if she's a girl or not, because I know she'll do really well. I'm going to make her the center of my team's offense." That really cheered me up.

Coach Staib was a good coach for me. He was able to figure me out. I'm not one of those people you can yell at, because I feel really bad whenever I think I made someone upset. Other coaches get in the faces of their players and scream at them, but Coach Staib didn't do that with me, even though he had been in the army and did that with a few of the other players. He figured out pretty fast that the best way to teach me was just to talk to me. He'd show me film and ask me what I could have done differently, and I'd learn from that.

Coach Staib lives close to me, and I knew his son, Joshua, who was on the team too. Joshua and I became friends. One time I went over to their house the day after a game to play with Joshua. When I was there, Coach Staib told me, "Just know that when I'm a coach I have to be a coach, but when I'm at home I'll still be a friend." He was probably getting me ready, because at the next practice he got really mad at us. We'd just lost a game, and we probably needed to hear it.

I'm glad I ended up with a coach who believed in me even though I'm a girl. Playing for a coach who really wanted me was better than being picked on a higher team. I wouldn't have chosen the B5 team at the time, but now I wouldn't change anything.

CHAPTER 5

Training My Sweet Feet

"Sam has a way of quietly inspiring
the other kids to play better."
——Chris Staib, Sam's coach

When I showed up for the first practice with my new team, I wasn't sure what to expect. I'd watched Max's practices, but every team is a little different. I also didn't know how the boys would react to me, but it turned out that the seventeen boys on my team were excited to have me as a teammate. I guess I'd already made a name for myself at tryouts, and while I wasn't happy to have fallen all the way to the B5 team, the other kids on the team loved it. They gave me tons of attention and waved and smiled at me a lot. Already, I felt like a bit of a celebrity, but I didn't think I deserved it.

Practice is a lot of work. For the first four weeks, we practiced two hours a day, six days a week. Even though it was early evening, it was really hot, and when you put on your helmet and pads during a scorching, dry Utah summer day, you feel like an egg

Coach Staib taught us about more than just football.

sizzling on a griddle. It's important to drink enough water so you don't get dehydrated. I don't always remember to drink water, but my parents make sure I do. My stepmom always sent me to practice with lots of water and Gatorade, and she and my dad constantly reminded me to finish it.

We had to buy the right kind of water bottle so I could drink through my face mask without taking off my helmet. Since I have such a small head, the normal chin strap that keeps the helmet on didn't keep it on me, so we had to hook it on a special way, through the helmet earhole, and put a longer pad on it so it could tighten up against my chin. Then we got a different chin strap that I had a hard time buckling by myself, which made it hard to get the helmet off, so it was a lot easier just to keep it on while I was drinking. If you watch videos of me, you might notice that I have to adjust my helmet a lot just to keep it from moving all over.

After two hours of running in full pads, my team was completely worn out. The next day we were still tired, but we had to do it again. Besides water, it's also important to eat enough food to have all the energy you need and build your muscles. On the way to practice, we'd stop at 7-Eleven and buy snacks, and usually I'd get a Dove chocolate bar. On the way home, we'd stop again. My stepmom also made sure I ate big meals. She got up early to cook breakfast, prepared a good lunch, and made a nice dinner.

Nobody could outrun me when we did wind sprints.

Brooke spent hours driving us around. Max had his football practice at the same time, but it was in a different place, and Ben and Annie were doing soccer too. It didn't help that my dad was often in Idaho for work. On most days my stepmom was out driving all of us around from about four o'clock to nine o'clock, without much of a break. We're lucky to have someone like Brooke.

About half our practice was spent just running and getting in shape. Sometimes we sprinted to the fence and back. Other times we did something Coach called "Helmets." He lined up our helmets and broke us into two teams. Then we did relays where each player had to carry the ball to the next helmet and run back before the next person in line could go. Since I was the fastest player, I was always the last one on my team to run, the "anchor." Tommy Hennigan, the second-fastest player, who Coach called "the Irish hitter," was usually the last one on the other team, and we both raced to see who would win. He always wanted to come in first, so it was always an intense competition, with the boys on both teams cheering us on.

At less than sixty pounds, I was probably the small-est player on the team, with only one other kid who was about my size. The biggest player was a boy we nicknamed "the Tank." As a nine-year-old, he weighed 152 pounds! During a drill where one player had to try to tackle another player who had the ball, the Tank had the ball and one of the bigger boys on my team tried to tackle him. The two boys collided hard, and one of them went down, but it wasn't the Tank. The other boy found himself flat on his back, aching. After that, Coach Staib made a rule that the Tank couldn't carry the ball during that drill. I guess he was worried somebody would get hurt.

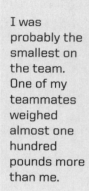

I was probably the smallest on the team. One of my teammates weighed almost one hundred pounds more than me.

One day we were doing that same drill, and Coach said, "Okay, one more time, and then we'll quit."

I really wanted to try to tackle the Tank, so I volunteered to be the tackler. "Can the Tank be the runner?" I asked Coach.

He wasn't so sure about that, but I guess he was a bit curious to see what would happen and let me try it. When he blew the whistle, I launched myself at the Tank and knocked him to the ground, even though he weighed almost three times as much as I did. I'm not sure how he reacted, because I just got up and walked away before he could do anything. After that, I think the rest of the team had a new respect for me.

We had another drill called "Deer Hunter." Coach gave each of us a Nerf football, and we started throwing them at each other. If you got hit, you had to sit down, but if you caught the ball, the person who threw it at you had to sit instead. Since I'm so quick, I was really good at dodging balls and usually was the last one standing, at least until the other kids started teaming up to get me out.

Sam's Vital Statistics

- **Name:** Samantha Anne Gordon
- **Height:** 49 inches
- **Weight:** 58 pounds
- **Birthday:** February 21, 2003

After we finished our different exercises and drills, we spent the last hour practicing—thirty minutes of offense and thirty minutes of defense. There was a lot to learn. You had to know where to run and what to do on each play. We started the season running five different offensive plays, and in most of them I ran with the ball. On each play, the blockers cleared a different hole that I ran through. When I was the one running with the ball, Coach liked to call a play called a "sweep," which meant that I'd run around the end, toward the sideline. He did that to take advantage of my speed, hoping that I could outrun the defensive players to the edge. I think he was also worried about me getting hurt if I ran through the middle, since that's where the biggest kids played. Anyone who weighed seventy-five pounds or more was called an "X-man" and could only play in the middle.

Sometimes Coach Staib would get upset at the blockers if they didn't do everything they could to make a clear path for me. That was because in practice I was able to get past the tacklers really fast and fly down the field, so the blockers didn't feel like they needed to really block. Instead, they'd get in the way of the defenders just long enough to slow them down. I guess they figured that was all I needed and didn't want to work too hard, since practice is hard enough anyway. Coach wouldn't let them get away with that, though. He wanted everyone to play with all the effort they could give.

I felt like there was a lot of pressure when I was playing on offense. My position was halfback, but since the ball went right to me, I was like a quarterback, except that I ran with the ball and didn't throw it. Since I almost always had the ball, it seemed like everyone was depending on me to make the play. If we didn't do well, I felt like it was my fault. And the hikes made me nervous! I'd stand three steps back from the ball, and a teammate would "snap" the ball to me, which means that he'd throw it through his legs to me the moment I said, "Hike!" Sometimes the ball was way over my head or really low, and I had to catch it.

Inspiring Women

"I am building a fire, and every day I train, I add more fuel. At just the right moment, I light the match."
—Mia Hamm, retired world-renowned soccer player

"I want that woman, that female, to know that she's no less than the stars in the skies. She's just as good as the guys. . . . She shouldn't think of herself as any less."
—Vivian Stringer, Hall of Fame basketball coach

Every once in a while, though, I missed the ball. Once it even bounced off my helmet! There was one time when I dropped the ball, which ended up on the ground before I was able to pick it up. Our blockers were headed toward one side of the field, so the other team went that way too, thinking that was the way I was running. After I grabbed the loose ball, I noticed there was nobody left on the other side of the field and just ran that way. I managed to go all the way for a touchdown, even after how badly the play started out!

As much as people focus on my offensive skills, I

like playing defense better. There's less pressure on me as the center of attention. It also feels good to tackle a bigger kid to the ground even though I'm one of the smallest players—and a girl. The boys usually don't say anything after they get tackled by a girl. They just get up and walk away.

On defense, I usually play cornerback, which is what most of the smaller kids play. That means my job is to make sure the person with the ball doesn't get around the edge. Defense really feels like a team effort. I can do my job even if I don't tackle the offensive player. All I have to do is work with the teammate next to me to trap the runner so he can't get through. Then the runner has a choice to try to get by me or go toward another player, and we can stop the run on our own or together.

Playing together was something Coach really tried to teach us. He said that if we work hard, believe in ourselves, and play as a team, we'll do well. I think he wasn't just talking about football, either—it seemed like he felt the same way about almost everything in life. And learning that kind of thing is more important than winning a football game.

Coach Staib is great. There's another coach for older kids who hasn't lost a game in five years, but he's known for yelling at his team and using bad words. Coach Staib isn't like that. Sometimes he would get mad at us—and we probably deserved it—but he almost always stayed

I was the only girl on my team, but that didn't matter to my teammates. I'm number 6 on the left end.

positive and motivated us by complimenting us when we did a good job. Instead of yelling, he'd usually just give us tips and tell us how we could do better.

Coach made me one of the three captains of the team, which meant that I would go out on the field for the coin flip that would determine who got the ball first. It also meant that the kids would make a circle around me during warm-ups and I'd tell them how to warm up. The captains were supposed to be role models for the rest of the team and make sure they were having a good experience playing football. There was a kid who was feeling pretty bad because he thought he was the worst player on the team. We all liked him and didn't want him to be sad, so when we were warming up for a game, I told him I thought he'd make a great captain and asked

him to take my place for that game. Being the captain made him feel good about himself. He played his best game that day!

After the season started, on Fridays we did something special to reward the team for playing hard the week before and motivate us for the next game, which was on Saturday. Coach gave out treats to three "Bull-dozers," who were the players who'd done the best blocking in the last game, and three "Bone Crushers," who were the best tacklers in the game. After that, Coach did something inspirational to get us excited for the upcoming game. Our first game was against the Wildcats, and I remember Coach giving each of us an Orange Crush soda and having us yell that we were going to "crush" the Wildcats.

Coach had us do different cheers to motivate us. We'd yell, "Whose day is this? Ours! Whose field is this? Ours! Who are we? Mustangs!" He also led us in spelling "Herriman" while doing jumping jacks. At the end of the season, he gave us chains we could wear around our necks with a medallion hanging on the end. On the front, the medallion said, "Whose day is this?" On the back it said, "Ours," along with "Gremlin B5."

With all this practice and motivation we were ready for the season to start. We even played a practice scrimmage against another team each Saturday to get a feel for what a real game would be like. As that first game got closer and closer, I got more and more excited. And nervous.

CHAPTER 6

Up, Then Down

"Talk about vision! Cutback ability. Burst.
Tackle breaker. Stops on a dime. Changes direction.
Makes people miss. Sam Gordon is amazing!"
—Mel Kiper Jr., ESPN

Game days are a big deal. We have to show up an hour and a half early to warm up and get ready. Some of the fields we play on are a long way away, and between the driving, the warm-ups, and the game itself, we are gone for four hours or more each Saturday. Max also has football games every Saturday, in different places, and Ben and Annie usually have soccer on Saturdays too, so weekends are really busy at my house.

My dad is my biggest fan. Before the season started, he decided to hire someone to film all our games. He got the idea because all the parents had chipped in to shoot Max's team's games the year before, and every week the team could watch the video and figure out how to play better. People could also put highlights together and post them on YouTube to share with family and friends. My teammates' parents weren't hiring anyone to film our games, so Dad stepped up and paid for it himself.

Even though we were just kids, the competition was fierce. Coaches sent people to record other teams' games so they could use the footage to prepare for games against those teams later in the season. I remember a few times my dad helped record games of teams on our schedule. Other times, coaches swapped film of teams they'd already played to help each other get ready. Coach Staib watched the videos to see our opponents' strengths and weaknesses in prior games so we'd know what to do against them.

With all that preparation and competitiveness, there was a lot of pressure, especially for a starting quarterback like me. I didn't want to let my team down, and I was really nervous going into that first preseason game. But it was awesome! Not only did I score a touchdown on my first carry, but I scored five times. I got the ball on eight plays, which means I only had three runs that didn't go all the way to the end zone! Coach Staib wanted to make sure my teammates had a lot of chances as well, so he didn't use me on every

Coach and the parents did a lot of things to get us excited for the games, like making banners for us to run through.

play. That was good because it was so hot outside that I got tired a lot faster than I expected. It was afternoon in August, and the temperature was over one hundred degrees. The track around the field was so hot I could feel it through my shoes.

Despite the heat, we won big in our first game. I was so glad I didn't make any big mistakes. It also looked like we had a really good team. We played well on both offense and defense, and my teammates blocked hard for me so that I could get free. Plus, they made some great defensive plays to stop the other team. I was really excited for the season!

I scored five times in my first game, even though I carried the ball only eight times.

The next game was the first one that counted, and it was a pretty good one too. I scored on the first play again, but it didn't count because there was a penalty. After that, I only scored one touchdown that counted, and it was the only one our team managed, so we didn't get nearly as many points as we did in our first game. A touchdown is worth six points, and then you get to try a conversion. In the pros, they kick the ball through the goalpost, but in Gremlin leagues, you can try from two yards away from the end zone for one point, or you can try from a little farther away for two points. After we scored our touchdown, we lined up for a one-point conversion, and I got the ball again. I was tackled just short of the goal line, but I reached the ball across. On the replays, it's hard to tell if I actually made it, but the officials thought I did.

That conversion ended up being the difference in the game. We held the other team scoreless until the end of the game, when they got a touchdown. They decided to go for a two-point conversion, which meant that if they made it, they'd win the game. My heart was really pumping for that play, which would decide who won. As soon as they snapped the ball, I burst forward and found myself in the backfield, along with my teammate. The ball carrier had nowhere to go, and we tackled him before he could even get going!

After a finish like that, we were wired! We'd now won our first two games, including the first one that counted. It seemed like we were pretty good.

The third game started out great too. I scored three times in the first half, and by halftime we were up by two touchdowns. But the second half was another story. On the opening kickoff, the ball went to the other side of the field from me. I wasn't anywhere near the play, which was over anyway, when a player from the other team hit me from the side with a cheap shot. When you watch the replay, it looks like his coach or a parent told him to try to hurt me on purpose. There was no reason for him to be going after me since the play was over when he hit me, and I was nowhere near the ball. The officials didn't see it, but my coach was *really* upset.

After that, our team fell apart. I guess we were emotional and distracted. That cheap shot didn't hurt me too badly, but a different hit did. As I was going out of bounds, someone hit me in the back with his face mask. It was just below where my pads ended, and it really hurt, causing a bruise that ended up lasting for days. I sat out for a while to recover before I came back in.

We just lost our focus—and the game too. That was a really disappointing loss. It was our first one, so we weren't used to the feeling of losing, and to be ahead by so much and then collapse made it even worse.

The entire next week, I was sick with a virus and

Sometimes getting tackled hurt, and so did losing.

felt pretty awful, but it takes something more serious than a little flu to keep me home from football practice. I didn't want to miss practice and not know the plays we ran during the next game, so I still went. Being sick slowed me down, which meant that Tommy Hennigan was outrunning me in practice. By the time I showed up to play on Saturday, I was still feeling awful. I barely made it through pregame warm-ups in the roasting sun, but I didn't tell Coach I wasn't feeling well. I was going to be tough and be there for my team.

That was the worst game of the season for me and for my team. We were playing another team from Herriman that we'd already beaten in scrimmages before the season started, so we thought we could win.

But we didn't get the easy win we were expecting. The B7 team really wanted to win, so they practiced hard and played tough. I just didn't have it in me that day. I couldn't make it around the end—the defenders would run me down and tackle me. On one play, Coach put me in to punt the ball, and I kicked it so low it bounced off my teammate's back right to me. I caught the football, and the other team took over right there. Once, Coach called a passing play, and I threw an interception that the other team returned for a touchdown. I didn't score at all the whole game. Coach figured out I was sick and made me sit out the entire fourth quarter to watch my team lose.

That was a hard loss to swallow. Now our record

included only one official win and two losses. This wasn't how I wanted the season to go. I felt terrible because I'd played so awfully. I guess Coach noticed that, because he came to my house after the game to ask if I was okay.

"No," I said. "I feel like I let my team down."

"Sam," he said, "everyone gets sick sometimes. Everyone has a bad day. It's okay."

Maybe I'm just too hard on myself, but it didn't feel okay. Having Coach come to my house and tell me that did help a little, though. It was good to know my coach wasn't mad at me.

I was determined I wouldn't let my team down again the following week. I was going to bounce back. The whole team was going to bounce back, if I had anything to do with it. We all practiced extra hard that week.

At the next game, we played a lot better, but we were still down by one touchdown. With time running out, we had the ball really close to the end zone. But then we couldn't get the last few yards to cross the goal line. We failed on four tries, so the other team got the ball back. We were devastated to come so close but not score. Our heads were all hanging down. Nobody was smiling.

But there was still some time left, and the other team had to run a play. They were backed way up against their own end of the field. The quarterback pitched the ball back to the runner, but he dropped the ball in the end zone! One of my teammates jumped on it, and the officials signaled that we'd just scored a touchdown! My entire team was jumping and celebrating. Coach Staib ran across the field, hopping up and down and pumping his fist.

After we punched in the conversion, the game ended in a tie, which meant we were going to overtime. In overtime, you get four tries to score, and after each team has had four tries, whoever is ahead wins. We got the ball first and scored a touchdown, then added a one-point conversion. We were all excited and hopeful. Could we actually pull out the win? It was sure looking like it.

Then the other team scored a touchdown too. Instead of a one-point conversion, they went for two, which meant they were going to either win or lose the game— no more ties. We tried our best but didn't stop the conversion. We lost by one point. Our emotions, which had been so high, dropped to disappointment again.

Even after that bitter ending, we felt a little better after that game because it had been so close and the finish had been so exciting. We felt like we played way better than we had the week before. With a little more improvement, we would come out on top.

The next game was the first one against a team from our division, which meant it was important to win if we wanted to take the division championship. Even though all the teams in our division were supposed to be the same level as the Herriman B5 team, some had won a lot more games than others. Our opponent was Alta, which was one of the best teams. We had to play a lot better if we were going to win. And we desperately wanted to win.

If anything, we played worse. The game wasn't even close. We kept turning the ball over, starting with the opening kickoff. By halftime, the game was out of hand, and it didn't get any better in the second half.

There were no smiles after that game. We'd lost four in a row now, and we were devastated. This wasn't how we wanted the season to go. Since we were now playing against teams in our division, if we were going to turn things around, we needed to do it now.

Breaking Barriers

"The best thing about women's tackle football is breaking barriers. We're going against gender norms."

—Liz Sowers, wide receiver for the Kansas City Tribe of the Women's Football Alliance. The Women's Football Alliance is a North American full-contact league with sixty-three teams, including the Utah Jynx from Sam's home state.

CHAPTER 7

Turning It Around

> "Gridiron sensation Sam Gordon, perhaps the most
> unstoppable player on any football field."
> —Alec Baldwin, actor and NFL Honors host

Coach Staib sat down with my dad to figure out what to do. "We need a win," Coach told him. "Nobody's happy." They had a spreadsheet with the statistics from every play so far that season, and they examined it carefully to figure out what changes could be made to help us win. That's when Coach Staib decided I needed to get the ball more—maybe even almost every play. He thought that would give us the best chance, and he figured my teammates wouldn't feel bad about not having as many carries if it meant we'd get the win. Anything was better than losing more games. That's not what we'd all signed up for.

But it wasn't that simple. The kids who weigh seventy-five pounds or more (the "X-men") all played on the line, so Coach had been running me to the outside and away from the bigger boys. He was trying to protect me, since I'm so small. Now, he told my dad,

"If I give her the ball every play, and if she always runs to the outside, the defense can just put most of their players on the outside. We'll have to send her up the middle sometimes. Are you okay with that?"

My dad asked me how I felt, and I was just excited to carry the ball more, so he told Coach he was fine with it too. We practiced that way all week and added a play where I ran up the middle. I was nervous because I knew there would be even more presure on me. If we didn't win, I would feel like it was my fault.

Giving me the ball more wasn't the only change Coach wanted to make to get ready for the next game. He decided we needed to have more fun, so he started being more positive and complimenting us when we did something right instead of being hard on us when we did something wrong. He even brought a stereo to the game so that we could listen to music while we warmed up. The Herriman High School mustang mascot showed

My blockers would lead the way for me. They don't get enough credit.

up and danced to the music. By the time the game started, we were fired up and ready to go. Somehow this game felt different from the last few. For some reason, we all felt more confident. It was time to prove that we were better than we'd shown the last four weeks.

All the changes worked. The first time we got the ball, we scored a touchdown. It took thirteen plays, and I ran the ball on every single one of those plays. By the end of the game, I'd gained about 350 yards. That's a lot for one game. I also scored several touchdowns, including one on a kickoff return. The other team just couldn't stop us.

We were on cloud nine after that game. It was good to see everyone smiling again. Nobody complained that I got the ball on almost every play, even though I felt a little bad for the kids who didn't get a chance with the ball. But we didn't win just because of me. My teammates did a great job blocking, and our defense was good too. Football is a team game. You either win as a team or you lose as a team. By this point in the season, we'd all learned that.

We were all thrilled with the win, but it was just one game. Could we keep up the winning ways?

The following week, we moved the ball up and down the field and I racked up yards and touchdowns. But the other team matched us touchdown for touchdown. Neither team could stop the other.

That team had a really good player who carried the

ball a lot. He was big and he was fast. At the end of the game, we were ahead by only one touchdown, and he had the ball. He broke through our defense and was sprinting down the field. I took off after him, and it became a footrace. Somehow, I ran him down and tackled him to save the touchdown and the win. That was close! But with two straight wins, we were starting to feel a lot better about ourselves.

That game was the first time anyone tackled me by grabbing my ponytail. My parents had tried everything to get my hair to stay inside my helmet, including a lot of different ways of braiding it. But nothing worked. That's okay, because when my ponytail flies behind me in the wind, everyone knows I'm a girl, and I like showing them what a girl can do. Being tackled that way hurt a little, but it only happened one more time.

There were only two games left in the season. Up next was Brighton. They hadn't lost a game. They'd even beaten Alta, the team that destroyed us. But if we won our game against them, we'd be tied for first place in the division! Alta had one loss in the division, to Brighton, and we had one loss, to Alta. If we beat Brighton, they'd have one loss too, and all three teams would be tied. It was a big game for us against a great opponent who had won all seven games so far. It felt like a big test. Were we going to continue our winning streak and prove we were one of the best teams, or were we just an average team?

I ran the opening kickoff back for a touchdown, and we never looked back. I ended up scoring three touchdowns, but one was called back because of a penalty, so I only officially got two. But that was enough, because they didn't score a point against us! We were really excited now—we'd beaten the top team in the division! Everyone was happy, and nobody minded that I was still getting the ball almost every play.

There was only one game left in the regular season. We dominated them and won by a lot of points. We had gone from losing four games in a row to winning four in a row! Alta and Brighton both won their games, so we finished the season in a three-way tie for first place. After what had happened earlier in the season, that felt really good. We were the comeback kids! We'd achieved our goal of winning the regular season division championship, even if we had to share it with two other teams.

Four teams made it to the playoffs, including us. The winners of the first two playoff games got to play for the championship title. Our first opponent was Alta, the only team from our division who beat us during the regular season. We felt like we were a different team now, though, and we wanted to prove it to them.

I also wanted to meet Alta's coach. A few days after the first time we played them, Coach Staib told us their coach was Luke Staley. He was a running back who played for my favorite team, Brigham Young University

I like to play outside, whether it's organized sports or just at the park.

My coach named me "Sweet Feet" because I can use my feet to make sure no one tackles me.

My decision to play football led to my joining the Herriman Mustangs Gremlin League team.

Gary Herbert, the governor of Utah, invited me to a Jazz game as a famous person who plays basketball in the Junior Jazz program.

My ponytail drew a lot of attention. There was only one other girl my age at the tryouts.

Meeting the US Women's soccer team was a dream come true. Here's me with Abby Wambach, Hope Solo, and Amy LePeilbet.

I got to be on the field while the New York Giants warmed up.

Coach Harbaugh from the San Francisco 49ers wanted me to make the 49ers my favorite team if they beat the Green Bay Packers.

Before the commissioner's press conference started, I got to stand at the podium.

I met lots of football players. This is Clay Matthews. He plays super tough on the field but is really nice in person.

I felt like a real celebrity wearing a fancy dress and walking the red carpet before the NFL Honors ceremony.

A seat like this at the Super Bowl could cost many thousands of dollars. The luxury suite was sweet!

I'm the first female football player to be on a Wheaties box! The box was unveiled live on *Good Morning America* with Josh Elliott.

All these celebrities I've met are really just regular people. Lucas Cruikshank and Laura Marano were great!

Snoop Lion (formerly Snoop Dogg) is a really nice guy. He coached his own son's football team!

(BYU), from 1999 to 2001. His yard and touchdown totals from his last year at BYU shattered school records. He was a consensus All-American and was recognized as the best college running back in the country. Before the season started, my dad and I watched some highlights of running backs to inspire me, and I was so impressed with Staley that I chose number 6 as the number on my jersey because that's the number he wore.

Luke Staley received awards for being the best running back in the country when he played for BYU.

I almost fell out of my chair when Coach Staib said that Luke Staley had called him after the game and said he was really impressed with me. My hero was impressed with *me*? Apparently, Staley mainly coached the offense, and when his team was on defense he'd take pictures, since his favorite hobby, besides football, was photography. He told Coach

Staib he was going to send me some of the photos he took of me and a note. A few weeks later, an envelope showed up at my house with some great pictures. You can find a lot of his photos in this book, including on the front cover. He also sent me some of his trading cards that he'd autographed, along with a personal note saying he was impressed with my football skills and with how hard I worked. That meant a lot, especially coming from someone like Luke Staley.

Praise from a Hero

"The thing that makes her special is [she's] a girl and she's the best in the league. I thought immediately of Barry Sanders, because of her speed, her quickness, and her ability to make people miss and run through people."

—Luke Staley, former BYU running back and Doak Walker Award winner

Even though Luke was one of my heroes and I was grateful for the photos and cards, I was still planning on destroying his team. We watched a lot of video of Alta's past games and thought we'd figured out how to win. But they were watching film of us, too, and they changed the way they were playing to try to stop us—to stop me, specifically. They shifted the people who played on the defensive line, and we found out afterward that their coach had told them to focus on

Luke Staley's son played on his team and was probably the best player in the league.

me. If I faked a handoff to someone else, they weren't supposed to fall for it until it became absolutely clear that I didn't have the ball anymore.

Their game plan worked. The score was just as one-sided as the first time we played them. They went on to beat Brighton the next week in the championship game, so at least we can say we lost to the best team.

The outcome of the game was disappointing, but I was happy to meet Luke Staley afterward. He told me he thought I was awesome and had a great game. That wasn't really true, but I wasn't going to argue with him. His wife even asked if I could be on their team next year, and we all laughed. I had my picture taken with him, and I was excited to meet such a celebrity. Little did I know that I'd be meeting a lot of other famous people in the next few weeks.

Sweet Socks for Sweet Feet

During National Breast Cancer Awareness Month, some kids wore pink with their uniforms to remind everyone of all the people who suffer from breast cancer. Sam's parents bought her a pack of colored socks, and she wore the pink ones. The next game, she wore fluorescent orange socks, then fluorescent green, followed by fluorescent purple, until Coach Staib suggested she stop wearing bright socks, since teams were already targeting her. "Why make it easier for them to track you down?" he said.

CHAPTER 8

Fame in a Flash

"So many people are marveling at her speed and skill, not because she's a girl playing a male-dominated sport, but because she's so completely dominating all the boys."
—Josh Elliott, *Good Morning America* anchor

Before I even got to the door on my way home from school, Max came running outside, yelling, "Sam, the *Ellen* show wants you to be on TV! They want to do a story about you!" He was talking about *Ellen* as in *The Ellen DeGeneres Show*. It didn't seem like he was teasing me, so it must have been true! I was shocked. Somebody wanted me to be on national television? Me! My dad explained that the producers weren't sure if they could do it or when they could do it, but that didn't make me any less excited. I couldn't believe a national TV show had even watched my video, much less liked it enough to want me on their show.

Someone from *Ellen* called only hours after we'd posted my highlight video on the Internet. My dad had been working on two videos throughout the season. One had highlights from the entire team, and he was going to give a copy to each player. The other had highlights of just me. It took a lot of time to load the film of each game on his computer, convert it into a format he could edit, put the clips together, and add music, but he was dedicated enough to get it done. Our season ended on Saturday, and by the next Tuesday the video of my highlights was ready to go. It was about four minutes long, with exciting music. Dad thought people would be interested in watching a girl dominate the boys, so he suggested that we put it on YouTube.

Tuesday morning before school, I sat down with my dad and we uploaded the video. Dad figured it would be cool to spread the word about the video, so I wrote a short post for CougarBoard, which is an Internet site where people can chat about BYU sports. I titled my post "My Story about #6 Luke Staley." Then I added the photo of me with Luke Staley, told about how I got to meet him, and inserted a link to my highlight video. After that, I went to school.

This photo of me with Luke Staley is what I included when I posted my highlight video.

By the time I came home from school, *Ellen* had called, and a lot of Internet sites were writing about my video and including links to it. My post on CougarBoard became the Post of the Day and ended up with over fifteen thousand views and lots of comments. People were saying that the video was awesome, that I run like Luke Staley, and that I'm lightning fast. By the time I went to bed, my YouTube video had been watched by over fifty thousand people.

When I woke up the next day, I found out that *Good Morning America* was going to be in town that day to film me for a show the following morning! After I'd gone to bed, my dad got a call from them. They were excited and wanted to do their own story. Dad told them *Ellen* was already interested and had wanted to do an exclusive interview, so he'd have to talk to the producers before he could commit to anything.

Good Morning America called back bright and early at six thirty on Wednesday morning. "Have you seen how many hits the video has now?" they asked. Of course, Dad hadn't checked that early in the morning, but they said it had two hundred thousand views by then. They really wanted to do something with me, they said. After that, they kept calling about every half hour.

So Dad called the *Ellen* producers back. They still didn't know when they could have me on, so they said to go ahead and do *Good Morning America*, and they'd get back to us about doing something, maybe the next week.

At one o'clock in the afternoon—the day after I'd posted on CougarBoard—the *Good Morning America* crew was at our house to film. I had to miss school.

They interviewed me and my dad at home and even talked to some of my teammates to put together a piece for the next morning. The story included a lot of my highlights too.

The next morning, my dad and I had to get up at five o'clock a.m. so we could talk to them over Skype— live on their nationally televised program, which has millions of viewers! Josh Elliott, one of the anchors, interviewed us. I was really tired from getting up so early, so I don't think I looked or sounded my best. During the live show, Carli Lloyd called in and told me to "keep working hard and keep dreaming." I thought I *was* dreaming—I was on national television and talking to a two-time Olympic soccer gold medalist! Of course, I was so tired that I didn't really figure out what was going on until Carli Lloyd hung up, and then I was kicking myself for not saying something to her that made any kind of sense.

Still, I'd just been on national TV with my dad! My whole family was really excited. We couldn't talk about anything else. None of us had ever imagined that posting those highlights would lead to this kind of excitement.

Nothing ever worked out with *Ellen*, but a lot of other opportunities came up. Later that same day, I did an interview with *Inside Edition* for a show that ran that night. There's a studio in Salt Lake City that we went to for the filming, so we didn't have to go out of town. They used a background that made it look like we were outside, even though it was just my dad and me in a small room, talking to a camera, with little speakers in our ears so we could hear what they were asking us. The *Inside Edition* people had already talked to Coach Staib and some of the Herriman Mustang players.

It was awesome to see myself on TV! That was something I'd always dreamed of: being on television and becoming famous. And now, in just a short time frame, millions of people had watched me on two different TV programs. I never thought playing football would lead to that!

A CougarBoard Sensation

Here are some of the comments posted on the CougarBoard site after Sam uploaded her jaw-dropping highlight video:

- "This is beyond AWESOME!"
- "Holy smokes . . . you are FAST!"
- "Lightning fast."
- "You have skills!"
- "A little Luke Staley, only faster."
- "Holy moly! Toughest little chick ever!"
- "Post of the century! Sam, you are my hero!"
- "I think this is the best thing I've ever seen."

Within three days, my highlight video on YouTube had been viewed almost five million times! I was surprised that so many people had seen it, all from just one link on the BYU message board.

I didn't go back to school until Friday. When I got there, my friend Kaydie ran up to me and yelled, "Sam, you were on TV!" She and one other girl had watched me. Everybody thought that was really cool, and they all wanted to know if that was why I'd missed school. That was probably the first time I felt really famous— the first time somebody said they saw me on TV. It was fun to feel like a celebrity, but it was nice that all my friends still treated me like the same old Sam.

By this time, my dad was getting flooded with calls from reporters and producers. My dad posted the video on YouTube with his law firm's account, so the media were all calling his firm. Now his four-person staff was busy almost full-time just taking calls about me, and my dad was even busier at it than they were. It wasn't possible to do all the interviews people wanted; we had to respond just to the national media. We felt bad, but we just didn't have time for everyone.

And there were quite a few national organizations calling. On Saturday night, I went with my grandpa, my dad, and Max to a BYU football game, where we met with the NFL Network and BYUtv. The night before, it snowed more than a foot, and Max's team played that morning, slogging through the white powder. That was their division championship game, and they won! In fact, they won their two playoff games by a combined score of 83 to 0. Going to the BYU game felt like a celebration of his success too. I might have been the one the media wanted to talk to, but Max accomplished more with his team, and I felt like he deserved a lot more recognition. Fortunately, he's such a good brother that he's never seemed jealous of all the attention I get. When he caught a glimpse of himself on one of the TV programs about me, he got really excited.

I got to go down on the field while the BYU players were warming up. Since I couldn't talk to any players before the game, I stood close by number 47, Ziggy Ansah, who was the fifth overall pick in this year's NFL draft.

The NFL Network and BYUtv had both arranged to have a film crew meet us before the game. We went to a pizza place with the NFL Network film crew, which was a lot of fun. Then we got to the game early and were able to go out on the field and hang out with the team while they were introducing the seniors for their last home game, which is called Senior Night. I got to meet some of my favorite BYU players, like J. J. Di Luigi. That was an awesome experience. A few BYU fans asked if they could take a picture with me, so I posed with complete strangers. Even the game was great—BYU crushed the University of Idaho.

There were only two downsides. First, the game was late at night and it was really cold after that big snowstorm. Second, they made me wear makeup for my BYUtv interview, and the NFL Network even showed me putting it on. I don't like wearing makeup—it makes me feel fake.

The next day, the NFL Network people came over to my house to do some more filming. They recorded me throwing the ball, even though I almost never threw during the season, and when I did I threw more interceptions than touchdowns. Luke Staley also showed up at my house to be filmed, and he brought his son, who had played for him on his Alta team. His son was probably the best player in the league, but Luke Staley was nice enough to say that I was. He even compared me to Barry Sanders, one of the best runners in the history of the NFL. Who could have imagined that? Luke Staley, at my house, saying such nice things about me!

My little brother, Ben, and my little sister, Annie, wanted my autograph, so I signed a picture of myself. They kept their copies next to their beds.

People were even starting to ask for my autograph—including my own family. I signed a photo my grandpa had taken at one of my games, and my dad made a bunch of copies that I could give away. The first two went to my younger siblings, Ben and Annie, and they both put them right next to their beds. I was a celebrity even with my own family!

By this time, I felt like I was living in a dream. All these amazing things, happening to me! I sometimes wonder how things might have turned out differently if we had made different choices. What if we hadn't moved where we did? What if I hadn't decided to play football? What if I'd ended up with a different coach?

Or on a different team? It's impossible to know what might have happened, but I was enjoying what did happen. And there was a lot more to come.

Sweet Tweets, Part I

These are some of Sam's thousands of Twitter followers:

- **Roger Goodell**, NFL Commissioner
- **The San Francisco 49ers**
- **Stuart Scott**, ESPN
- **Sam Ponder**, ESPN
- **Alex Morgan**, US Women's National Team (soccer)
- **Abby Wambach**, US Women's National Team (soccer)
- **espnW**

CHAPTER 9

Tour of Fame

"Sam, you're one of my favorite people I've
ever interviewed here on *SportsCenter*."
——Hannah Storm, ESPN

Hey, are you Sam Gordon? Sweet Feet?"
     I couldn't believe it. A complete stranger had
just recognized me. I was at the Salt Lake International
Airport to fly to Chicago for yet another TV show, and
I was wearing my Herriman Mustangs football jersey
with "Gordon" in block lettering on the back.

Pretty soon, there was a crowd of people around
me, asking for photos and autographs. Wow. That must
be how real celebrities feel. It felt pretty good.

"Hey, Sam?" This time it was one of the Southwest
Airlines employees. Several of them were in the crowd
asking for photos. "Will you sign our Wall of Fame?"

I had no idea what that was, but I said yes. He got
the security supervisor to clear me to go back to the
employee break room, and there it was: a wall with
celebrity signatures on it, all from rock stars and actors
and other really famous people who had come through

I couldn't believe the airline employees wanted me to sign their Wall of Fame.

the Salt Lake International Airport, like NFL Hall of Famer Steve Young and rapper Snoop Dogg (now Snoop Lion). It was amazing to me that they thought my autograph belonged on that wall! I was thinking, "Oh my gosh, this is awesome!" I was a real celebrity!

That flight was just the first of many. During the month after my *Good Morning America* appearance, I spent more nights in hotel rooms than in my own bed. I saw places like Chicago, Los Angeles, San Francisco, and New York. I'd had a taste of stardom already, but

nothing like what was about to happen on my whirl-
wind tour of the country. I loved having the opportunity to see lots of places I'd never been before. Luckily,
we were on break for most of this time, so I didn't miss
too much school.

Before I left for Chicago, I had an interview with
Fox & Friends, a cable news talk show. That meant
my stepmom and I had to get up at four thirty a.m. to
be at the studio in Salt Lake on time—the same studio
where I did *Inside Edition*. *Fox & Friends* sent a car
with a driver to pick us up, and I was shocked when a
limousine pulled up in front of our house. It wasn't too
fancy on the inside—no TV or Jacuzzi or anything—
but I still felt like a real celebrity as the chauffeur drove
us to our destination.

This was the first time my stepmom was on TV with
me, and she was nervous. She's shy to begin with, and
when you put her on national television, she gets really
tense. Since I'd done it a few times already, I told her
just to pretend she was talking to her best friend, and
I think that helped. For some reason, I don't get very
nervous on TV. Put me in front of my fourth-grade class
for a spelling bee and I'm a wreck. Tell me my football
team is counting on me, and I worry myself sick. But
put a camera in front of my face and broadcast me to
the world, and I feel totally fine. I know it doesn't make
sense, but that's how it is.

I was so tired for *Fox & Friends* that I didn't look very

good, but at least I got to hop back in that limo when I was done. This time, it took us to the airport to catch a flight to Chicago, where I was going to be on *Steve Harvey*. That's when everyone started recognizing me and wanting me to sign things like the Wall of Fame.

After I signed the Wall of Fame, the Southwest Airlines employees insisted that we go to the beginning of the line and board before everyone else. I felt guilty cutting in line, but it also felt really cool. The flight attendants were excited that I was on their airplane. Some of them took photos of me. Others texted their kids to tell them they'd just met Sam "Sweet Feet" Gordon.

When we landed, that kind of treatment didn't stop. A limo showed up to take Brooke and me to a real luxury hotel. We were walking through the lobby when the concierge said, "Hey, cool jersey, kid!" Then he did a double take. "Sam? Sam? Is that you?"

He ran over to us, blurting, "I just watched your video on YouTube! It's you! It's you!" He had us take a picture with him, and then he made us wait while he ran to get us two glasses of milk and a plate of cookies. I couldn't believe complete strangers were recognizing me, even in Chicago!

We had time to see some of the sights in Chicago while we were there and to try the food. Chicago-style hot dogs are awesome. They load them up with mustard, pickles, ketchup, and relish. There's so much stuff they have to use a toothpick to hook it all together. I don't like tomatoes, though, so I took them off. But Chicago-style pizza isn't nearly as good as their hot dogs. There's a Chicago-style pizza place near my house, but I've never liked it, so I thought they didn't make it right. I was wrong. I didn't like the real thing either. They make it really thick, with the cheese under the sauce.

We saw Chicago's Navy Pier, where we almost froze to death, then went to the top of the Willis Tower, the tallest building in the United States. On the 103rd floor, over thirteen hundred feet above the ground, there's a walkway with a glass bottom so you can see all the way down. We took pictures there at the top. It was really fun and terrifying at the same time. How lucky could I be? I got to see a new city, and my parents didn't even have to pay for it!

The day after we got there, we did the filming for *Steve Harvey*. This was probably the first time I was nervous for any of my interviews. I was going to have a live studio audience for this one, but that wasn't why I was worried. It had more to do with my decision to do something a little crazier than normal. They wanted me to show them a football move during the show, and I decided to take that a step further and do a touchdown celebration dance I like to call my "Sam Dance." I didn't get to use it during the football season because it's against the rules to celebrate, but I thought it would be fun to do.

Everything turned out fine for *Steve Harvey*. I acted silly on national television, but it was fun. I showed them how to tackle, and then I did my dance. Some people told me I was really cute, so I guess I didn't look as silly as I thought I might. Steve Harvey gave me some Chicago Bears and Green Bay Packers stuff and asked me if I was a Chicago Bears fan. I told him I hadn't been but I was after his show.

After we got home from Chicago, I got to spend two days at home before Brooke and I left on Saturday for Los Angeles so I could appear on the NFL Network again. This time it was a live appearance on *NFL GameDay*, which is a show they do on Sunday morning before all the football games start. I was on the set with Marshall Faulk and Warren Sapp, former NFL players who are both in the Hall of Fame, as well as former NFL head coach Steve Mariucci. Since Warren Sapp was a defensive player, he had me show him some of my football "jukes" while he tried to tackle me. He missed, but that was probably on purpose. I'm glad he didn't tackle me, because he's enormous! Then, since Marshall Faulk was a running back, they had me tackle him while he tried to get away. It was so much fun!

After *NFL GameDay*, a car service took us straight to the airport so we could fly to the San Francisco area, where the San Francisco 49ers had invited me to attend a Monday Night Football game. After the Green Bay Packers, the 49ers were my favorite team, so I was excited. We got there on Sunday to watch their practice with some of the families of the players. The food at the 49ers practice facility was great. They have a big cafeteria with a lot of choices, including hamburgers, macaroni and cheese, and a bunch of different treats. They even have a chef who will make you just about anything you want.

The team took us on a tour of their exercise and practice facilities, which are really nice and big. I got to hang out with some of the players (who were also really big) while they were practicing, including Colin Kaepernick, who was going to start his first NFL game on Monday. Of course, nobody knew then that he would lead the 49ers all the way to the Super Bowl. Colin was really nice, and he even threw the ball back and forth with me for a while. He seemed a little overwhelmed and excited that he was going to get his first start. I could understand how he felt, having just become an overnight star myself.

I met Colin Kaepernick the day before his first NFL start. He went on to play in the Super Bowl.

I also got to meet LaMichael James, who asked me to sign his hat, and I led the team in a cheer where we yelled, "1, 2, 3, 49ers!" The players all autographed a football for me. The 49ers' coach, Jim Harbaugh, talked to me for a while, and he asked me who my favorite team was. I told him the same thing I told Steve Harvey: the Packers are my favorite, the 49ers my second, and the Bears (who the 49ers were playing the next day) became my third. He said he'd make me a deal: if the 49ers beat the Packers in the playoffs, they'd become my favorite team. I told him, "Okay." The 49ers eventually did go on to beat the Packers in the playoffs, but the 49ers would have become my favorite team even without my deal with Coach Harbaugh.

On Monday, my stepmom and I had some time to see San Francisco before the game started, so we walked to the ocean, which took about an hour and made us so

I led the San Francisco 49ers in a cheer.

tired that we didn't spend much time there and ended up taking a taxi back. We never made it to the Golden Gate Bridge, but we did see the most crooked street in America, which was pretty cool. It wanders back and forth up a hill in a crazy way.

That night, we got to the game early and went on a special tour of the stadium and the field. Then I got to be part of the ESPN pregame show. They put a desk on the field, and I sat behind it next to Steve Young, Stuart Scott, and Trent Dilfer while wearing a custom 49ers jersey with my name on it. That was really cool, especially since Steve Young played for my favorite college team, BYU, before he started his Hall of Fame career with the 49ers. I answered some questions for the show, then went up to my seat with my stepmom. Our seats were incredible—right at the 50-yard line and almost in the front row. There was even a snack bar there with cupcakes and other treats.

I got to hang out with Steve Young on the Monday Night Football pregame show.

At halftime, they showed a clip about me on the big screens, and then I ran out onto the field in front of sixty-nine thousand fans! I waved at everybody, and they cheered for me. But then I wasn't sure what I was supposed to do, so after a moment I just ran back to the sideline. After that, everybody knew who I was, and tons of people wanted pictures of me, so I did my celebrity pose a lot. With all that attention and the 49ers winning the game by a lot of points, it was a great night.

Sweet Tweets, Part II

Sam has been one of the top ten topics trending on Twitter on four different occasions. Here's what some sports stars tweeted about Sam:

- **Barry Sanders:** "That video is impressive. Looks like I've found a girlfriend for my nine-year-old."
- **Brandon Marshall:** "Lil Sammy is a beast."
- **Desmond Howard:** "The Heisman race is wide open. . . . Sam Gordon is my front runner right now."
- **Mia Hamm:** "Sam Gordon's video on *The Today Show* was sick! You go, girl!"
- **Pete Carroll:** "Saw Sam Gordon's film and wow!"

The next day, Tuesday, we were back on an airplane. This time, we flew to New York City. Our hotel was right in Times Square, so my stepmom and I walked around and checked out all the bright lights.

The following morning, which was the day before Thanksgiving, I was on *Good Morning America* again, live on set instead of over Skype. This time, an executive from General Mills was there for the unveiling of a new Wheaties cereal box with me on it! That's right: I'm the first female football player ever to be on a Wheaties box. Underneath my picture, it says, "Sam Gordon: Football Star." That's a big honor, because Wheaties only chooses the best athletes, like Michael Jordan, for their boxes. The unveiling of the box happened outside in Times Square, and Josh Elliott, the anchor, picked me up for most of the time he talked to me, so we could both fit in the same camera shot. During the interview, I was so overwhelmed that I couldn't say anything except that it was awesome. I couldn't believe it! Just a few weeks earlier I was still playing football in Utah, and now here I was in New York on national TV with my own Wheaties box!

As if that weren't enough, they told me right after I was on *Good Morning America* that ESPN wanted to interview me on *SportsCenter* with my Wheaties box. The interview was supposed to be real quick—like a minute—but the person who interviewed me, Hannah Storm, was really fun to talk to and we talked for almost ten minutes. We talked about football, being a girl playing against the boys, and my love of soccer. At the end of the interview, she even told me I was one of her favorite people she'd ever interviewed on *SportsCenter*. That meant a lot to me because Hannah Storm is a big name when it comes to women and sports; she's one of the first women to be a TV sports anchor.

In just one week, I'd been to Chicago, Los Angeles, San Francisco, and New York City; met Hall of Fame football players; practiced with the 49ers; attended a Monday Night Football game; gotten a Wheaties box with my photo on it; and appeared on *SportsCenter*. Now, I was heading home for Thanksgiving, thinking that my little taste of fame was probably over. I had no idea what was still to come.

Sweet Feats

Here are some of the honors Sam has received so far:

- First female football player to be featured on a Wheaties box
- Cartoon Network Hall of Game: Most Viral Video
- Top 50 Most Googled Female Athletes of 2012 (according to TotalProSports.com)
- The Jane Dough's 50 Women of the Year (2012)
- Utah "Best of State" Female Amateur Athlete
- South Jordan, Utah, proclaimed December 18 "Sam Gordon Day"

CHAPTER 10

A Dream Come True

"Sam, you're my new hero, I just want to say."
— Gretchen Carlson, coanchor of *Fox & Friends*

When I got home from New York for Thanksgiving, I had the best news waiting for me: Abby Wambach from the US Women's National Team—the best woman soccer player in the world—invited me to come to one of her games! In some of my interviews, I said that she was one of my biggest sports heroes. Abby heard that and contacted me using Twitter. She wrote, "Sam Gordon, heard u were a fan. I am one of yours. Get in touch with me, and I'll fly you and a parent out to a game before Xmas. Sound good?"

Sound good? I'm not sure "good" is strong enough. Try amazing, awesome, or wonderful! I had just gotten home from a pro football game and a tour around the country and couldn't believe that things could get any better, but now they had.

The only problem was that I didn't even know what Twitter was, much less how to use it to talk to Abby. So my dad and I got on the computer and started learning about Twitter so I could answer Abby and tell her I'd absolutely love to come to one of her games. After I set up my Twitter account and tweeted back to her, something awesome happened: Abby followed *me* on Twitter. My very first Twitter follower was Abby Wambach herself!

Abby invited me to a game the week after Thanksgiving. But before that, I had Thanksgiving and a fun vacation planned.

We got home the night before Thanksgiving, and in the morning, my photo was on the front page of the *Salt Lake Tribune*'s largest paper of the year! Lots of people pay attention to the Thanksgiving paper for the ads, so now it seemed like everyone in the whole state knew who I was! That was a big surprise, because we hadn't had time to set up an interview with them.

After checking the newspaper, I played football, of course! It's a family tradition to play football on Thanksgiving morning. Then we eat a big, home-cooked Thanksgiving meal with pie for dessert. Like most people, we like to rest after dinner, but this year was different. We had to leave right after dinner to go out of town again.

This time we were headed to a soccer tournament I was playing in. It was in St. George, Utah, which is about a five-hour drive from my house. I had a blast at the tournament with the other girls on my soccer team. We've been playing together as a group for a long time, and they are my very best friends. I really missed them when I was playing football. All our families stayed at the same hotel, so when we weren't playing soccer, we got together to eat pizza, swim in the pool, and watch movies in our hotel rooms.

And we didn't do too bad in our tournament games either. We won our first three games but lost in the championship game—to a team we'd already beaten.

After the tournament, I stayed on the move. On Sunday, we drove back to Salt Lake City, did a little laundry, packed, and then went straight to the airport to catch a flight to California, this time for a family vacation to Disneyland. Since I was off school for a break at this time, we'd planned this vacation months before. Of course, back then we had no idea that I'd be doing so much other travel.

We stayed at Disneyland for four days and rode every ride at least once. It was awesome. My favorite ride was California Screamin', which is a big roller coaster that goes really fast and upside down. I went on that ride over and over again.

Since my stepmom had gone with me around the country the week before, my dad got to come with me to Phoenix for the US Women's National Team soccer game. We flew straight from Los Angeles to Phoenix on Thursday night. Once again, no time to go home. But I didn't care because I was so excited to meet all those amazing women. Abby Wambach had even invited me to come to their practice the day before the game.

Abby got us a room at a fancy hotel near the stadium, where all the players and coaches on the team were staying. When we got there, we kept looking out for the players, but we didn't see any because it was late. In the morning, we went shopping for some new soccer cleats I could wear during practice, since mine didn't fit anymore.

Then I had an interview with KSL, which is a Utah television station. When we told the sports anchor for their news program, Tom Kirkland, that we couldn't do an interview at their studio because of all our travel, he wasn't discouraged. He volunteered to come meet me in Phoenix so KSL could be the first local station to interview me. He brought a cameraman to do an interview and follow me around a bit at the US Women's National Team practice.

After the KSL interview, I met the US Women's National Team press officer in the hotel lobby to head on over to the stadium. But he wasn't alone. Sydney Leroux and Amy LePeilbet, two players from the team, came with him to escort me to their practice at the University of Phoenix stadium!

We walked over to the stadium together, and when we got there we threw the football to each other for a little bit. Then, when we got to the field, they invited me to kick a soccer ball with them. I asked them to teach me some moves, and they showed me how to just barely skim the ball and make it roll forward with a spin. I even got to kick the ball into the same goal the US Women's National Team was going to use for their game.

Abby Wambach taught me a few soccer tips.

After Sydney and Amy gave me some good soccer tips, the rest of the team came out, led by Abby Wambach! Seeing the entire team come out of the tunnel together was impressive and intimidating, but I didn't get too nervous because they were all smiling and they're all so nice. Abby gave me a really cool gift: a US Women's National Team jersey with my name on it. It was even number 6. She said I was really lucky because no one other than the team's players ever gets their own name on a jersey. Even the players who try out for the team don't get their names on jerseys. But that's not all. She also gave me a jersey with her name and number on it. She and all the other players on the team signed that jersey.

Abby then invited me to warm up with her. I did

a warm-up run with her, and the other players were giving me high fives and yelling, "Go, Sam!" But once practice started I needed to watch from the sidelines since they were so good and so fast—and a lot bigger than me.

As I watched, I kept thinking, "I hope one day I can be as good as they are." When you see them up close, what they can do is even more impressive. I'd been to one of their games before, and I remember thinking, "I wish I could be down on the field with them." Now I was there, actually on the field! I hope that my other dream can also come true: that someday I can join them as a member of the team.

After an intense practice, we played a little football! Abby Wambach has a really strong arm, and she said she kind of wished she'd played football when she was little. So she had Sydney Leroux run really far away and then threw the ball all the way to her. I couldn't believe how far she could throw! And it was right on target every time.

I played football with the US Women's National Team. Abby Wambach has a great arm!

We also lined up in a football formation and played touch football to see if they could catch me. My favorite play was when I was the receiver, Megan Rapinoe was the defender, and Abby was the quarterback. I ran forward, faked left, and cut right. Megan went for the fake and got left behind, so I was wide open. Abby threw the ball right at me and I caught it. There were a couple thousand people in the stands watching the practice, and they all cheered when I made the catch. Maybe Megan and the others were just taking it easy on me, but it sure was fun.

The next day was game day. After going to a movie with my dad, we went to the game. Abby got me VIP tickets and a pass to go on the field after the game. The United States played against Ireland and won 2–0, with Alex Morgan and Megan Rapinoe both scoring goals. The score could have been a lot more one-sided, but the Ireland goalkeeper did a great job of saving a lot of goals. Afterward, I was able to go down on the field and hang out with the players again. I heard a lot of people say, "Look at her. Isn't she cute?" I chatted with Alex Morgan again, and we talked about the great game. I couldn't believe I was actually talking to Alex Morgan like she was my friend!

I also got to meet a lot of the players from Ireland, who were all super nice. One of the Irish players went out of her way to give me an autographed jersey and joked with me about how "football" meant soccer where she was from. Then she challenged me to a race down one of the locker room tunnels. I'm up for any challenge, even if it is a race against a professional soccer player. She was a lot faster than me, but she let me win.

I felt like I was floating for the next few days. On the flight home, I just couldn't get over it. I'd met the US Women's National Team in person and practiced with them. We'd even played a little bit of football together. As fun as Disneyland was, meeting Abby Wambach and the US Women's National Team was better.

Deserving of Fame

"Sam deserves every bit of fame she gets, because she's so grateful for it and realizes the opportunity this is for her."
—Alessandra Meyer, Sam's fourth-grade teacher

I had only been home for one day in almost three weeks. When this trip was over, I thought my life was finally going to get back to normal and that all the fun would come to an end. But when I got home from school on my first day back, my dad had two more big surprises for me: a company called Rio Tinto was paying for our entire football team to go to a Utah Jazz basketball game, and the man in charge of the entire NFL, Commissioner Roger Goodell, invited me to a Giants game in New York City because he wanted to meet me!

The Jazz game was on Friday and the Giants game

was on Sunday, so I couldn't wait for the weekend! Even the week of school was fun because I had a lot to talk about with my friends, and we were doing a lot of fun Christmas activities at school.

Rio Tinto invited my entire team to the Utah Jazz game because a lot of the TV interviews of me and my teammates were done in Rio Tinto parks. Rio Tinto is a mining company that owns one of the largest open pit mines in the entire world. The copper mine is so big, they say you can see it from outer space without a telescope. My home is close to the mine, and Rio Tinto developed the parks and trails in our neighborhood. They wanted to thank us for showing how beautiful our neighborhood is by inviting us and a parent to a game.

Since my stepmom went with me to the 49ers game and my dad went with me to the US Women's National Team game, I thought it would be awesome if my mom came with me to the Jazz game. Not only did we get to go to the game, but we also got to go to the warm-up shoot around before the game and meet the players and coaches. One of the coaches I met was a former player for the Jazz whom everyone kept calling "Horny." I thought that was weird until someone told me that "Horny" was short for his last name, Hornacek!

The Jazz game was fun, and a lot of people asked me for pictures and autographs, especially after they showed me on the big TV screen at the top of the arena.

When I went to the bathroom, one little girl kept following me around until she ran into her parents. She told them, "It's that person!" The best part of the game was when the Jazz's mascot, Bear, carried me around on his shoulders and let me spray Silly String.

I got home late from the Jazz game and had to wake up early the next morning to catch a flight out to New York City for the Giants game. But that was okay because I wanted to get to New York early enough that we could check out some of the sights. Our hotel was right near Central Park, so we set off walking. There were a lot of people riding in carriages pulled by horses as we headed to the famous toy store, FAO Schwarz. The line to get into the store seemed a mile long since everyone was shopping for Christmas. Then we walked to Rockefeller Center to see the really big Christmas tree and the ice-skating rink. The streets were packed with so many people! It was a lot of fun to experience New York at Christmastime.

After breakfast, a limousine showed up at our hotel to take us to the stadium. The limo took us right up to the stadium's front gate, and the driver told us he'd still be waiting right there after the game to take us back to our hotel. I've been to a lot of football games, and we usually have to park about a mile away and walk to the stadium and then fight traffic to get out. It was great to be spoiled by having a limo to and from the game.

We got to the game early and met the NFL's "PR

Visiting New York was really fun. I finally got to see the famous Rockefeller Center Christmas tree.

Guy," Brian McCarthy, who gave us a tour around the stadium that was really cool—even if you're not a big football fan like I am. Brian took us up to the press box and showed us the replay booth. There was a sign on the door of the booth saying that absolutely nobody could go in, but Brian works for the commissioner, so he can go anywhere he wants. When we went in, the replay official showed me how the instant replay works when they need to figure out the right call for a play that just happened on the field. The media press box was really nice too, and there was a lot of food there—kind of a cafeteria. Brian said that the most important thing the team could do to keep the media happy is to feed them good food!

Next, we went down into the tunnel leading from the locker room and watched as the players walked past onto the field. We even got to go onto the field while the teams warmed up. While we were there, we met some famous people, like comedian Jon Stewart, who was there with his son. We also met a former player—I don't remember his name—who had a bunch of Super Bowl championship rings that he let me try on, as well as Pam Oliver, an NFL sportscaster.

Finally, it was time for the game. Brian took us through some secret passageways in the stadium where we always had to flash our VIP guest badges to security before they'd let us through. Our seats were in Commissioner Goodell's luxury suite. From his suite, we had access to the Commissioner's Club, which is a fancy place with wood panels and impressive fireplaces. And the part I liked best: an amazing buffet with fancy foods like prime rib and seafood but also football food like hot dogs and popcorn—and even a candy buffet. It was all you can eat and drink. My dinner was hot dogs and Swedish Fish!

After I ate my food I got a hot cocoa and headed to our seats, which were outside, right next to the fans, because the commissioner likes to talk football with the fans. The commissioner brought his twin daughters and their friend, who are all about a year older

Commissioner Goodell spent a lot of time with me. He's in charge of the entire NFL.

than me. We sat next to them for the whole game and talked with them a lot. The commissioner and his family were very careful to make sure they didn't cheer for either team during the game. Even his daughters said they didn't have a favorite team. I guess when you're supposed to be fair to everyone in the league, it's important to stay neutral and not look like you're choosing favorites. The fans sure weren't neutral, though. They loved watching their Giants win by more than three touchdowns.

Brian met us early the following morning to give us a tour of the NFL headquarters, and that's when I decided I wanted to work there one day. It was awesome! Instead of carpet, they have artificial turf.

There's football memorabilia everywhere, including a wall with Super Bowl rings for every single Super Bowl champion. The conference tables are shaped like football fields with the lines drawn on them and everything. They even have a "water cooler," which has a bar with stools where you can get soda pop and watch TV, which, of course, was tuned in to football highlights.

Brian then showed us the workout facility, and as we were leaving, we bumped into Commissioner Goodell, who was heading in for an early-morning workout. When he saw me he asked me if I'd ever been to the Super Bowl before. When I told him I hadn't, he asked, "Would you like to?"

I nodded, and he said, "Maybe you should ask Santa Claus."

CHAPTER 11

A Super Celebrity at the Super Bowl

> "[Commissioner Goodell] thinks she is an inspirational story for football, youth football, and the participation of girls in sports."
> —NFL spokesperson Greg Aiello

Just after Christmas, a handwritten note showed up at our house from Commissioner Roger Goodell on official NFL letterhead.

It turned out that he was not just inviting me to New Orleans for Super Bowl XLVII, which is on a Sunday, but to his "State of the League" press conference the Friday before and to the NFL Honors awards show on Saturday. Not only was I going to the Super Bowl, but I was going as the NFL commissioner's special guest! A lot of media outlets thought that was big news and started publishing stories about my invitation.

But between then and the game, I did two more TV interviews. Fuji TV, one of the biggest television stations in Japan, came to my house to do a story about me. For some reason, they wanted to film my family eating dinner together. We hadn't cooked anything, so they recorded us eating peanut butter and jelly sandwiches.

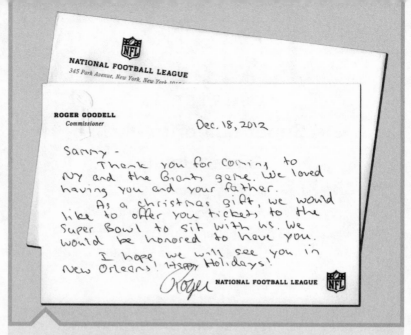

The best Christmas present ever was this invitation to the Super Bowl from Commissioner Goodell. He even took the time to write me a personal note.

We thought that was weird! I'm still not sure how that story turned out, since I don't speak Japanese, but I was amazed that people five thousand miles away actually cared about me, especially since they don't even play football in Japan.

For my next TV interview, it was back to New York City for the third time in two months. This time it was to meet Katie Couric and record a piece for her talk show, *Katie*. I was one of a handful of kids they brought in for a show they called "Katie's Wonder Kids." The other kids were experts at dancing, pool, piano, spelling, and martial arts. Katie talked to both me and my stepmom, and then she challenged me to a Nintendo Wii race. She quit before the race was over, and I won. I'm not sure if she quit because she was really tired, or if she was just taking it easy on me, but she was out of breath, so I think I really did win. What made the trip even better was that I got to see the musical *Wicked* on Broadway with Brooke. That was my first Broadway musical, and it was incredible!

The media attention didn't stop. Just before we left for the Super Bowl, I got a really cool invitation to be a guest blogger for espnW. They thought it would be a lot of fun for espnW readers to see what it was like for me to be at the Super Bowl, so they wanted me to write pieces for their Web site telling about my experiences. The first thing they wanted me to talk about was my travel to New Orleans. I'd done my share of traveling over the past couple of months, and I had it down. I always made sure my iPod was fully charged so I could listen to music and play games. I also took my backpack and filled it with some snacks and a book. So I had a pretty good setup as we flew from Salt Lake City to Atlanta, and then from Atlanta to Mississippi, where we stayed—about forty-five minutes from New Orleans, which is in Louisiana.

On the Friday morning before the Super Bowl, we drove to New Orleans for the commissioner's press conference at the Super Bowl media center. When we got there, I got my VIP pass so I could go anywhere I wanted. The media center was enormous and filled with different booths and attractions. Each major media outlet has its own display. One booth had a machine that embroidered hats. They found one in my size, with an NFL logo on the front, and sent it through the machine, which added "Gordon" in stitching on the side. I love that hat. There was also a green room where they take your picture and then add a background that makes it look like players are pouring Gatorade over you, like they do to coaches who win the Super Bowl. Cam Newton, a quarterback who won a college national championship and the Heisman Trophy before being the top NFL draft pick and the Rookie of the Year, was nearby, speaking to the media.

Cam Newton wasn't the only celebrity we saw. I got to shake hands with Clay Matthews from the Green Bay Packers. We also talked to Jim Rome, who has a popular sports radio talk show. He told me I was "the hardest act to book" and that he wanted to have me on his show sometime. Other people we met there included political commentator James Carville and Mallory Hytes Hagan, who is Miss America.

Next, we went to Commissioner Goodell's "State of the League" press conference. I got there a bit early and went on stage and pretended to make a speech! Then the room started to get packed. There were over a thousand reporters there to cover it. Before it started I met Tom Benson, the owner of the New Orleans Saints, who is really nice and asked me to sit by him, but I couldn't because the NFL had a special seat for me. I was one of five special guests the commissioner introduced during his speech. Other guests were people like the High School Coach of the Year. They also had the NFL players who had been nominated for NFL Man of the Year sit next to us, so I got to meet Larry Fitzgerald, Jason Witten, and Joe Thomas. They all seemed like great people, which makes sense because they were all finalists for an award recognizing their community service. After the press conference, the commissioner invited me up to the stage for a photo with him. I was feeling pretty special to get all that attention.

After the press conference we headed to the NFL Experience, which is like a theme park for football fans. It was in a huge convention hall filled with booths and

Mardi Gras is a big party they hold every year in New Orleans. The masks and costumes people wear are so wild.

NFL memorabilia. There were stations where you could get players' autographs, and in one place they showed all the footballs they've used in the Super Bowl. They also showed how footballs are made. I got to try lots of games; I raced against some high school basketball players and lost, I tested how far and how high I could jump, and I tried throwing footballs at targets.

After exploring the NFL Experience for a while, we headed to a rehearsal for the NFL Honors awards. That's the event where they announce the winners of different awards, like Most Valuable Player, Man of the Year, Rookie of the Year, and so on. It's on national television and is a really big deal. It took us forty-five minutes to get there, even though it was only two miles away, because of all the crazy traffic for Super Bowl weekend, but we made it there and I met actor Alec Baldwin, who was hosting the show. He was awesome—a nice guy and funny too. That's when they gave me some lines for a part in the show and asked me to try them out. I messed up the first time I practiced—I pointed the wrong way and mispronounced the name of the band I was introducing—but I got it right the second time. I was ready for Saturday night.

After the rehearsal it was my time to play football. I was invited to a ProCamps for kids to play football with NFL players. It was awesome! I got to play touch football with Darren Sproles and Mark Ingram of the New Orleans Saints.

Hanging with the Celebs, Part I

Here are some of the many entertainers Sam has met since she became an overnight star:

- **Alec Baldwin**, actor
- **Nick Cannon**, actor/comedian/rapper
- **James Carville**, political commentator
- **Katie Couric**, TV show host
- **Lucas Cruikshank**, actor and creator of *Fred*
- **Snoop Dogg, aka Snoop Lion**, rapper
- **Josh Elliott**, *Good Morning America* anchor
- **Mallory Hytes Hagan**, Miss America
- **Steve Harvey**, TV show host
- **Cast of *Incredible Crew***
- **Laura Marano**, actress and star of Disney's *Austin & Ally*
- **Bridgit Mendler**, actress and star of Disney's *Good Luck Charlie*
- **Jim Rome**, radio talk show host
- **Jon Stewart**, TV show host and comedian
- **Jerry Trainor**, actor and star of *iCarly*

On Saturday morning I had an interview with an ESPN reporter. She was really fun to talk to and we hung out at Café du Monde, drinking hot cocoa and eating beignets, which are yummy deep-fried French pastries covered in powdered sugar.

Roger Goodell and Alec Baldwin were fun to work with.

The Café du Monde is near Jackson Square, a famous tourist site with a lot of art and other things to buy. They even had fortune-tellers. So after my interview with ESPN, one of them read my fortune. She said that I was going to have three children and that someday I'll be a doctor. We'll see!

We walked down the famous Bourbon Street to a CNN interview, and by the time my interview was over, it was time to get ready for the NFL Honors show.

But first, I had to pick out a dress. I hardly ever wear dresses, and I had no idea what I should wear on the red carpet. Luckily I had some help from a famous fashion designer, Oscar de la Renta. Oscar de la Renta gave me six dresses to choose from . . . and I got to keep the one I picked! It was probably the first time in my life that I was looking forward to dressing up. But that doesn't mean I wore makeup—I didn't. Very few people ever have a chance to wear an Oscar de la Renta dress once, much less take one home! My stepmom wore a fancy dress too, and my dad was in a nice suit.

We hadn't eaten since the morning beignets, so we were hungry. We didn't know when we'd get to eat again, so we went to a deli to grab a bite. I ordered spaghetti and meatballs with buttered corn, and I thought my dad was going to freak out. He put napkins all over my designer dress so I wouldn't have a big tomato sauce stain across the front of me on TV. I still managed to get a small drop on me, but it wasn't in an obvious place, so it wasn't too embarrassing.

Now it was time for the red carpet entrance. There was an actual red carpet. It was really long, and it took a lot more time than I thought it would to walk down. Reporters were interviewing players, and photographers were taking lots of pictures. I felt like a real celebrity, walking in at the same time as Aaron Rodgers, the Packers quarterback who's a Super Bowl champion and a league Most Valuable Player. And we were sandwiched between two Hall of Fame greats: Steve Young and Jerry Rice. It's not easy to recognize football players when they aren't wearing uniforms with a name on the back, so I relied on my dad to tell me who a lot of the people were.

I felt like a movie star wearing my Oscar de la Renta dress while walking down the red carpet.

I got to sit with my parents for most of the show until it was almost time for my part, when they moved me to a chair next to Commissioner Goodell.

While I was changing seats, something really cool happened: they played my entire highlight video on the big screens in front of the best football players in the world and the most important people in football. You could hear the audience gasp, "Ooh!" and "Aah!" as I juked my way down the field or made a big hit on defense. When the video ended, the entire audience clapped really loud for me, and I couldn't stop smiling.

Then Alec Baldwin introduced me as "the most unstoppable player on any field."

Commissioner Goodell added, "Who knows, Sam. You might be the first woman to play in the NFL. Would you like that?"

I replied, "No. I'm coming after your job!" Everyone laughed!

"Commissioner Gordon," Alec Baldwin said. "I like the sound of that!"

Then I said, "But first I want to try something easy, like hosting an award show."

Alec Baldwin acted upset about that. He told me if it was so easy I should get to work hosting the show—and I did! I introduced the band OneRepublic, which immediately started playing a song.

During the whole skit, people were laughing, which made me feel good. But once I was finished, I ran as fast as I could to the bathroom. Famous football players and actors were giving me high fives and trying to stop me to talk as I ran up the aisle, but I was rushing by so fast that I didn't notice who they were. I wish I could have appreciated the moment a little more!

But that's okay because I got to meet a lot of the players and stars after the show. I had so much fun that night that I wasn't tired at all—just hungry. So we stopped at Chili's on the way back to the hotel and ate chips and queso, Diet Coke, and my favorite dessert, molten chocolate cake. By the time we made it back to the hotel, I was passed out asleep in the back of our rental car.

The next day was game day! The Super Bowl is by far the biggest American sporting event of the year. Once again, we got the VIP treatment: VIP parking, VIP security line, VIP tailgating, super VIP tailgating, and VIP luxury box seats.

We arrived a few hours before the game started so we could party! The tailgating party was separated into three big areas: a parking structure, the arena, and a big tent. The parking structure had four levels, with a different New Orleans theme on each level. For example, one was the "Jazz" level and one was the "Mardi Gras" level. The party had live jazz bands, fortune-tellers, live alligators, and lots and lots of food.

On one level of the parking structure, there was a crab race. I thought that meant real people would be doing a crab walk as fast as they could, but it turned out that they had hermit crabs racing against each other. Each crab's shell was painted different colors, and the race organizers had given them each a funny name. One was called "Crabbernick," as in Colin Kaepernick, one of the Super Bowl quarterbacks. The announcer told everyone that Crabbernick was taking the lead, while another crab was "taking a nap."

King cakes were popular at the party. I guess they're a traditional food in New Orleans, especially around Mardi Gras. They're a pastry that's kind of like a

The tailgate party was a blast. Every level had a New Orleans theme. This is a real live alligator.

cinnamon roll. For some reason they put a plastic baby on the bottom of one of the slices of cake. They say whoever gets the slice with the plastic baby will have good luck. But they also have to provide the cake for the next party. I was lucky and got the slice with the plastic baby on the bottom. I guess I'll have to make the cake for next year's Super Bowl party!

In the arena we got to watch a special concert with OneRepublic and Matchbox Twenty. Since the concert was only for VIP tailgaters, we could get as close to the stage as we wanted.

The tent was huge and had even more food, drinks, and live music. In one section of the tent was an even more exclusive area roped off for guests of the commissioner, and since I was one of his guests, we got in! Inside was more food and a lot of famous football players and team owners. That's where we had a chance to talk to Steve Young. His wife told me she thought I did great on the NFL Honors award show, and their sons wanted my autograph! I thought that was pretty neat that kids with a dad as famous as Steve Young wanted my signature!

As if getting into a VIP tailgate party wasn't enough, we got to sit in the best seats in the entire stadium to watch a game that over one hundred million people watched. Some very important people were sitting in the commissioner's luxury suite with us, but when we showed up, the commissioner made us feel like we were the most important people there. He told me how great he thought I did at the NFL Honors award show and said, "Sam, I'm going to make a TV star out of you. Alec Baldwin kept talking about you all night and how he'd love to do something with you!" That made me feel good and made me think maybe I could try a little acting!

I noticed that the commissioner didn't have a seat of his own; he was just there to make sure everyone else was having a good time. Nearby was Urban Meyer, the football coach at Ohio State University. Before going to Ohio State, he won two national championships as the coach at the University of Florida, and before that he led the University of Utah to an

Here's a close-up of our tickets to the Super Bowl. Some people paid lots of money to be there.

undefeated season. Since he'd lived in Utah for a while, he was excited to learn that's where we were from, but then we teased him that we were BYU fans. BYU and Utah are big rivals.

We sat with a lot of other famous people in our suite as well. There were football coaches like former Super Bowl winner Tony Dungy and national champion Les Miles from Louisiana State University. We met Dallas Cowboys star Jason Witten, as well as Hall of Famer Jim Brown, whom some have called the best professional football player ever. The coaches of the two teams playing the Super Bowl were brothers, Jim and John Harbaugh, and their parents were in the suite with us too. There were also some important political figures like Governor Chris Christie from New Jersey, US Secretary of Defense Leon Panetta, and US Attorney General Eric Holder. Because of those political people, the security to get into our suite was really tight—much tighter even than at megastar Beyoncé's suite.

The suites next to us had some big-time celebrities, like singer Beyoncé; rapper Jay-Z; model and actress Kate Upton; Neil Patrick Harris, the actor from *How I Met Your Mother* and *Doogie Howser*; and NBA coach Pat Riley. The sports and political figures in our box kept looking over at the stars next to them to see who was there, and those entertainers kept looking over at us to see who was in my box. It was as if there were two different worlds of famous people curious to know what the other world was like.

Valuable Seats

The highest-priced tickets for a suite at Super Bowl XLVII were $420,000. The cheapest seat was $850.

I really didn't spend too much time chatting with the celebrities because I wanted to watch the game. The first half of the Super Bowl was depressing for me. The 49ers were losing big. I was sitting there, disappointed, when Commissioner Goodell came over to sit by me for a TV shot. I perked up a bit while talking to him, which was good, because at that moment CBS played an NFL commercial with me in it, then showed me and the commissioner sitting together. Over one hundred million people saw me on TV!

A lot of people watch the Super Bowl just for the advertisements, and now I've been part of one. In the commercial, they called me a "forever trailblazer." A trailblazer is the first person to make a trail so that other people can follow. I guess they felt that when I played football so well against the boys, I was doing something no one had done before, and they believed other girls would do the same. I hope they're right!

Valuable Seconds

A 30-second commercial at Super Bowl XLVII cost an average of $4 million.

After that my parents' phones were going crazy with everyone they know sending them text messages saying they saw me and my commercial. Even the others in our suite were telling me they were getting text messages from their friends and family who saw me on TV.

I really enjoyed the halftime show, and it put me in a better mood. I went out into the hall after the show was over and walked right past Jay-Z. Beyoncé came up to the suites a few minutes later, and I could see her from where I was sitting.

Hanging with the Celebs, Part II

Here are some of the football stars Sam has met:

- **Victor Cruz**, wide receiver for the New York Giants
- **Marshall Faulk**, Hall of Fame running back
- **Jim Harbaugh**, San Francisco 49ers coach
- **Michael Irvin**, Hall of Fame wide receiver
- **Chris Johnson**, running back for the Tennessee Titans
- **Colin Kaepernick**, quarterback for the San Francisco 49ers
- **Urban Meyer**, Ohio State football coach
- **Les Miles**, LSU football coach
- **Jerry Rice**, Hall of Fame wide receiver
- **Aaron Rodgers**, quarterback for the Green Bay Packers
- **Warren Sapp**, Hall of Fame lineman
- **J. J. Watt**, defensive lineman for the Houston Texans
- **Steve Young**, Hall of Fame quarterback

In the third quarter, the power went out and they stopped the game for about thirty minutes while we sat in darkness. When the stadium got its power back, the 49ers got their power back too. Colin Kaepernick led the 49ers, scoring a bunch of points in a short time. With about two minutes left in the game, the 49ers, down by five points, moved the ball all the way to the Ravens' seven-yard line. I was thinking, "What a perfect finish!" I turned to my dad and said, "We've got this won."

I must have jinxed the 49ers, because I was sure wrong. After four failed tries to get into the end zone, they turned the ball back over to the other team and lost the game. But at least they made it exciting at the end. It was definitely an exciting end to the most exciting weekend of my life.

The NFL sure put on a great show in New Orleans for the Super Bowl.

CHAPTER 12

Partying at the Green Carpet in LA

"Sam Gordon looks like a cast member of *iCarly* but runs like Adrian Peterson."
—Heavy.com, *The Top 20 YouTube Videos of 2012*

The next weekend, I had another big event. Every year, the Cartoon Network broadcasts a show called the *Hall of Game Awards*, where they give out awards to sports players based on fan voting. I was nominated for Most Viral Player because my video had gone viral and been watched by millions of people. There were some other cool videos that had been nominated too, including a sixty-seven-yard field goal by a high school football player (longer than the NFL record), a community college baseball player making an incredible catch while leaping over the fence, and a ballboy at the Australian Open tennis tournament using lightning-fast reflexes to snatch a ball out of the air.

We arrived in Los Angeles a day before the show so we had time to meet a soccer player I met through Twitter: Caroline Stanley, who was the goalkeeper for the University of Southern California. Caroline invited me to the campus to meet her and the women's soccer team and tour the athletic facilities. The school facilities were amazing! Their weight room was almost as big as the 49ers'. They had an indoor football field, lounges for the players, and my favorite thing: underwater treadmills, where most of your body is underwater while you exercise. I wished I'd brought my swimsuit so I could try it out. If I can, I'm going to go back and give it a shot. I kicked a mini soccer ball around with the USC women's soccer team, and then we played some touch football, which was a blast.

The next day the Cartoon Network sent a limousine to pick us up and take us to both the dress rehearsal and the actual show. I really wanted to win the trophy! I'd watched the show before, and I knew it would be really cool. Since I knew the competition was stiff, I'd gone on CougarBoard, sent out tweets, and posted on Facebook, asking for people to vote for me. And they did. At the dress rehearsal, I learned that I'd won the Most Viral Player award by millions of votes! They wanted me to rehearse my acceptance speech, which they wrote for me. But I asked if I could give my own speech, and they said I could.

The Hall of Game Awards were held in an empty airplane hangar, which was pretty cool. On the way in, instead of a red carpet, they had a green carpet, but it felt the same: like a dream. The media was taking pictures as we walked in, and I ran into Colin Kaepernick again. He remembered me and said hi with a big smile on his face. If he was disappointed by narrowly losing the Super Bowl, it didn't show. Instead, it seemed like he was just as amazed by all the attention he was getting as I was.

Colin Kaepernick remembered me! We both became instant stars at about the same time.

At the show, I met even more celebrities. Like Colin Kaepernick, some of them were the sports players who had been nominated for awards, like NFL stars Victor Cruz, Chris Johnson, and J. J. Watt. We sat next to J. J. Watt, who was really nice and really big! Other famous athletes we met included Olympic swimmer Ryan Lochte (one of my stepmom's favorites), sprinter Allyson Felix, and WNBA basketball player

Swin Cash. Swin and I had a lot of fun making funny faces together.

Hanging with the Celebs, Part III

Here are some of the sports figures Sam has met:

- **Swin Cash**, WNBA player
- **Kate Fagan**, ESPN reporter
- **Allyson Felix**, Olympic sprinter
- **Roger Goodell**, NFL Commissioner
- **Ryan Lochte**, Olympic swimmer
- **Jane McManus**, ESPN reporter
- **Shaquille O'Neal**, former NBA basketball player
- **Stuart Scott**, ESPN anchor
- **Hannah Storm**, ESPN anchor
- **Abby Wambach, Hope Solo, Alex Morgan, Carli Lloyd, Sydney Leroux, Amy LePeilbet**, and **Heather Mitts**, US Women's National Team (soccer)

Besides the sports stars, there were other celebrities there. Since this show was on Cartoon Network, it was aimed at kids, so I recognized the famous people a lot more than I did at other places we went. I got to talk to rapper Snoop Lion, who used to call himself Snoop Dogg; Lucas Cruikshank, the boy who created and does the voice of the cartoon character Fred; Bridgit

Mendler, who writes and sings songs and plays Teddy Duncan in *Good Luck Charlie*; Jerry Trainor, an actor who has performed a lot of famous roles, including Spencer Shay on *iCarly*; and the cast of *Incredible Crew*. Laura Marano, who plays Ally Dawson on *Austin & Ally*, presented me with my award, with the help of J. J. Watt. And, of course, Shaquille O'Neal and Nick Cannon hosted the show. Shaq is so much taller than me that it was hard to fit both of us in a camera shot.

At over seven feet tall, Shaquille O'Neal is really big! He was a cohost of the *Hall of Game Awards*.

When they announced I was the winner, I raced up the ramp and ran over two guys in yellow outfits, knocking them to the ground. Then J. J. Watt handed

Nick Cannon, who was the host of the *Hall of Game Awards*, created the *Incredible Crew* TV series. I got to meet the whole *Incredible Crew* cast.

me the trophy, which is really heavy, and picked me up so I could give my speech into the microphone. I said I had dreamed about having a Hall of Game trophy on my bedroom wall, and now my dream was coming true thanks to Cartoon Network and everyone who voted for me. I really meant it! I really did want that trophy. And now it really is in my room.

After the show, we moved to another airplane hangar for an after-party. There was a DJ and lots of food—things kids love to eat, like corn dogs, peanut butter and jelly sandwiches, a bar full of candy, and another bar with all different colors and kinds of Goldfish crackers. We talked to a bunch of the celebrities, and there were also a bunch of games. My favorite was the spinning gyroscope ride, which went fast and almost made me throw up. But that didn't stop me from riding it over and over!

The ride was sort of like my life for the last several months; it was fast and made me dizzy, but it sure was a lot of fun.

The Same Sam

"Sam is a humble person. I think she gets a little shy and uncomfortable because of all the attention. She hasn't changed at all. She's still really sensitive and caring."

—Brooke Gordon, Sam's stepmother

CHAPTER 13

Riding the Wave

> "Sam will succeed at whatever she does.
> She can be whatever she wants. She has
> the drive and the intelligence that it takes."
> —Chris Staib, Sam's football coach

I thought things would quiet down after the Super Bowl and the Hall of Game awards, but the attention hasn't stopped. We're still getting calls from TV media and others, like *Sports Illustrated*. I was invited to another Utah Jazz basketball game with our governor to announce "Junior Jazz Day" because I play in the Junior Jazz program. I also had the chance to go to a Real Salt Lake soccer game and have a conversation with their mascot on Twitter. Now I have thousands of Twitter and Facebook followers, including a bunch of famous people. It just goes on and on. I never dreamed my story would get so much attention.

Since I don't know where the fame will take me, I'm working hard to make sure I have a great future outside of football. Football is great, but my real passion is soccer. My dream is to play soccer with the US Women's

Reaching my goal of playing soccer with the US Women's National Team will take a lot of hard work.

National Team, so I'm practicing as much as I can. And to prepare for life after soccer—whether that's in ten years or thirty—I'm being as good a student as I can in school. I really love animals, and I'd like to own a pet store when I grow up. Maybe I'll start by working in the pet training area at Petco when I'm in high school. That sounds really fun. And even before that, maybe my dad will let me get a dog. He told me he would if I juggle a soccer ball with my feet two hundred times without dropping it, so I'm practicing!

Becoming famous and meeting a lot of famous people has been a lot of fun, but sometimes it's nice to just be anonymous for a while. The great thing is that when I don't wear my football jersey nobody recognizes me and I become an ordinary kid again. I'm sort of like Hannah Montana. When she's Hannah, she's a big star, but when she's Miley Stewart, she's just a regular person. I'm kind of the same way: when I wear my jersey, I'm Sweet Feet and people want my autograph, but when I take it off, I'm just Sam Gordon again. It's almost like magic.

I've also discovered that being famous is about more than just enjoying the spotlight. It also gives you an opportunity to inspire people and do some good in the world. PBS and AOL put together a documentary called *Makers: Women Who Make America*. It's about women trailblazers who overcame obstacles so that the rest of us can follow in their footsteps. During the documentary, they showed a commercial with me in it that called me a "maker" on the football field. The commercial said that makers are people who are "defining our past, impacting today, [and] shaping our future."

A True Student Athlete

"Sam is not just a good student, but a good person. She made friends in the class and many looked up to her."

—Linzi Pettey, Sam's third-grade teacher

Compared to the barriers the women in the documentary faced, I haven't done anything special. They're the ones who paved the way for girls like me. These women were told they couldn't vote, they couldn't play sports, and they couldn't be important government officials. There weren't a lot of people who tried to stop

This is my winning science project! To prepare for life after sports, it's important to me to do well in school.

me from playing football. These women's efforts made it possible for kids like me to do things girls never used to be allowed to do.

Pioneers in Women's Sports

"Perhaps it just comes down to my parents not letting me feel like I was any different or like I should give myself different standards because I'm a girl. Maybe by being who I am and what I've done so far it will change the mindset within families, and parents will point that out to their kids and let them know that they can do whatever they want."

—Danica Patrick, first woman to win an IndyCar race

I guess in some ways, maybe I'm paving the way for others too. Because of courageous trailblazing women, there are a lot of girls playing most sports, many of them in all-girl leagues, but football is still an exception.

Even today, there are people who won't let girls play football. A little while after I started being famous, there was a news report that an eleven-year-old girl, Caroline

Pla, had been banned from playing in her football league in Pennsylvania after she had played (and pretty well) a full season. She was breaking the rules that entire season because her league didn't allow girls to play, and now they were saying she couldn't play the next year.

An online petition was started up to let Caroline play football the next season. I posted something on Twitter asking people to sign it. There were some people who wrote to me saying that girls shouldn't play football with boys and even saying some mean things, but a few weeks later, the petition had more than fifty thousand signatures. *The Ellen DeGeneres Show* picked up the cause too. And not too long after that, the league decided Caroline could play after all!

That's when I realized I can make a real difference. And that's why I'm sharing my story. Just like there are more and more girls playing soccer, I hope football will become a sport for both boys and girls. And just like there are now soccer leagues for women and girls all over the country, maybe one day there will be opportunities for girls to play football in their own leagues. I'd really like that.

People tell me my story is about a lot more than making a difference in football, though, and even about more than just sports. When I went to the San Francisco 49ers game, there was a group of cheerleader girls my age who really wanted to meet me and have a photo taken. They thought I was awesome. I was kind of embarrassed by that, but I guess they saw me as an inspirational figure. Most likely, none of them will play football, but they still found something about me that they admired. I feel like a normal kid who's just doing something I love, but if that inspires other people to have the courage to achieve anything they want in life, that's a good thing.

Jump on It

"I think every athlete has their window of opportunity, and you just have to jump on it. You never know when it can end."
—Hope Solo, US Women's National Team goalkeeper

When I decided to play football, I knew I was in for a big challenge, but I had no idea what kind of wild ride it would be. Playing football was a lot of fun, and writing this book has been a great way to relive this incredible year full of amazing experiences. I'm glad I played football, and who knows what the future holds. I hope there are lots more exciting things to come, and I'm working hard to do my best at everything I do. And maybe I can even find new ways to inspire people while I'm at it!

In sports and in anything else, I think girls shouldn't be afraid to do things that mostly just boys have done.

You don't have to be a man—or even a Tommy

I was just trying to blaze through defenses, but people say I was blazing trails for others. Winning feels good, but inspiring people feels even better.

boy—to be an engineer, an accountant, a computer programmer, or a construction worker. But my story's not just for girls, either. The boys on my basketball team think what I've done in football is amazing, and they're glad to have a girl on the team. Whether you're a boy or a girl, you shouldn't be afraid to go for whatever you want to achieve. Not everyone has sweet feet, but everyone can accomplish sweet feats.

Sam's Dreams for the Future

- **Occupation:** Pet store owner
- **Education:** College at a place with a good soccer team
- **Sports goal:** Olympic soccer team

ACKNOWLEDGMENTS

My football success was possible because I had great people supporting me along the way. My older brother, Max, never went easy on me and taught me to be tough. Max's coach, Jason Fife, let me run speed drills with his football team and planted the seed in my mind to play when he took me to the side and encouraged me to play. And I couldn't have done it without Coach Staib and my Herriman Mustang teammates— go Mustangs!

My dad and I sat down together before the season started to watch highlights of a great running back, Luke Staley, and never imagined that we would actually get to meet him one day. Thanks, Luke, for being an inspiration and for letting us use your photo of me for the book's cover!

Abby Wambach is my hero, and it was awesome to meet her and the entire US Women's National Team. I was so excited she agreed to write the foreword to this book. Thanks, Abby! And a big thank-you to her agent, Dan Levy, and to Aaron Heifetz with the US Women's National Team.

I can't say enough about how great NFL Commissioner Roger Goodell has been to me. I had the experience of a lifetime at the Super Bowl. Thanks also to our friend at the NFL, Brian McCarthy, who took us to the New York Giants game and showed us around the NFL headquarters.

Thanks, Bob Lange and everyone with the 49ers for inviting me to San Francisco—I'm a 49ers fan for life!

If it looked like I was having fun during my media interviews it's because I *was* having fun! Every single person I met, whether a producer, a reporter, a cameraman, or a host, was really great to me.

When my dad was swamped with hundreds of phone calls from the media, a number of people volunteered their time to help manage the craziness, including publicist Ariane Sloan and attorneys David Eklund and Maritza Schaeffer. We would have been lost without you. Thank you!

I had a ton of fun hanging out at the kitchen table with my neighbor Ari Bruening, reliving my football season. Ari came up with the vision for the book and did a lot of work putting my story on paper. James McGinniss is the literary agent who believed in the book and made it happen. Cindy Loh, the publishing director at Bloomsbury Children's, caught the vision and put her team to work. Mary Kate Castellani is an amazing editor, and she is backed up by a talented group of publicists, copyeditors, and others. Lots of people let us use their photos. A big thank-you to them.

And finally, the biggest thanks to all the BYU fans on CougarBoard who shared my highlight video with the world!

SAMANTHA "SWEET FEET" GORDON is a ten-year-old football sensation who made international headlines by crushing the competition in a league of boys. She gained celebrity status when her football highlight reel reached almost five million views on YouTube in just three days. Since then she's appeared on more than seven hundred TV programs, including being in a Super Bowl commercial and on ESPN, *Good Morning America*, and Cartoon Network, and has thousands of Twitter followers. Sam lives with her family in Utah.

@Sam_Gordon6
Facebook.com/SamGordonFootball

ARI BRUENING is an urban planner, an attorney, a writer, and an avid football fan who graduated magna cum laude from Harvard Law School. A friend of Sam Gordon's family, Ari lives in Utah with his wife and three children, who he hopes are inspired by Sam to believe they can do anything they want in life. This is his first book for young readers.

PHOTO CREDITS

Used by Permission